Life's a Cavalcade

LIFE'S A CAVALCADE

GLEN MICHAEL

Foreword by
MARK MILLAR

BIRLINN

First published in 2008 by
Birlinn Limited
West Newington House
10 Newington Road
Edinburgh
EH9 1QS

www.birlinn.co.uk

ISBN13: 978 1 84158 750 9
ISBN10: 1 84158 750 8

British Library Cataloguing-in-Publication Data
A catalogue record for this book is available from the British Library

Typeset by Carolyn Griffiths, Cambridge
Printed and bound by MPG Books Limited, Bodmin

Contents

Foreword

Most people get invited to write an introduction. Not me. I pretty much forced myself on these poor sods.

Flash back one year and I'm in the pub with some friends and one of them, who works with Birlinn, tells me that they have just secured the rights to Glen Michael's autobiography. The excitement from the whole table was palpable. Glen, after all, was like a member of the family for three entire generations of Scottish children. Growing up in the Central Belt, he was our third parent on Sunday afternoons, sandwiched between *Farming Outlook* and Arthur Montford.

The moment you heard those familiar chords ('Day Out' – I looked it up) you knew it was time to drop your Chopper, your Grifter, your BMX, your Evel Knievel Stunt-cycle, your Tiny Tears, your football, your Buckaroo and your Swingball, your Boglins, your Chic-a-Boo, your Rubik's Cube and your Remus Play-kits. It was time to stop playing and start watching because Glen Michael was coming on.

I've tried to explain the significance of this show to my ten-year old daughter, but in an age of countless channels repeating non-stop cartoons, a show that could only promise fifty minutes of cartoons a week sounds a little disappointing. But context is everything, and at a time when animated shorts were only used to fill five-minute gaps in the TV schedule *Cartoon Cavalcade* was Cathode-ray Heaven. This could be an urban myth, but I've heard people say it was the one hour a week in the '70s and '80s that not a single Glasgow nipper was hit by a car because the streets were cleared for Bugs and Daffy.

Posh kids watched *Swap Shop* on BBC and the rest of us watched *Tiswas*, but Glen's show appealed to boys and girls in equal measure, young and old, rich and poor. It was a communal experience and touched three different decades before Glen and his lovely wife Beryl took the show to a new generation as they toured the schools and entertained the kids in person. The variety of the format is what appealed to me most. It was impossible to get bored, between Glen's sketches, the characters he created or even the birthday slot where (pathetically) I have to 'fess up to sending in drawings several times a year in the hope of hearing my name read aloud on STV.

Most significantly for me, *Cavalcade* was my introduction to superheroes and Marvel Comics. I first met Spider-Man during one episode and, encouraged by older brothers, started snapping up the books and drawing my own comic-strips. Glen was the catalyst between Coatbridge and Gotham City. He brought these guys into my living room every Sunday, and it's no exaggeration to say that if he hadn't taken what he thought was a little short-term gig back in the '60s I absolutely wouldn't be in Hollywood now. Chatting recently with other Scots working in LA, everyone's face breaks into a smile when I mention that I'm writing this introduction. James MacAvoy put it quite succinctly when he said it was the one time on television where you heard a Scottish accent and an American accent on the same show every week. Glen taught us to broaden our horizons.

Of course, he's embarrassed when I mention this, and looked a little surprised when I asked him to be the Guest of Honour for the UK premiere of my movie *Wanted* in summer 2008. But even though I've worked with some of the most beautiful women in the world and some of the biggest-name actors these past few years, I've never seen such excitement in the company of a celebrity as I saw on the faces of my friends and family when they met Glen at the premiere. For a moment, they forgot all their adults concerns. For a few minutes, they were ten years old again and beaming as they lined up one by one to have their photographs taken beside him, transported back to long, hot Sundays, soup bowls filled with scoops of ice-cream and tins of mixed fruit cocktail. It's a powerful thing to be in our living rooms in our formative years, and this is why, back in the pub, I strong-armed my way into writing this introduction. This was my chance to say thank you.

Of course, there's more to Glen than a single cartoon show. He's an old-school entertainer trained up in an era where you didn't get famous by doing six-week stints on reality TV arguing with your fellow crazies. As you'll see from the book, he's done his years in military service, played music halls with some of the country's most famous entertainers and is an accomplished actor in his own right. I almost choked on my supper a while back when I saw him, eyes wide and skinny as Jimmy Stewart, as Jack Warner took a slug from Dirk Bogarde in *The Blue Lamp*. Glen Michael is perhaps one of the most famous brand names in the Scottish entertainment industry and yet, when we pause to think, we really know so very little about the man.

But, with *Life's a Cavalcade,* that's all about to change.

Enjoy the book.

Mark Millar
Glasgow
August 2008

Mark Millar is a multi-award winning author and has been the UK's highest-selling comic-book writer working in America for the past decade. He has worked on everything from Spider-Man comics to the Iron Man *movie and most recently wrote and produced* Wanted, *starring James McAvoy, Angelina Jolie and Morgan Freeman. He works as a consultant for Marvel Comics in New York, but lives with his family in their native Scotland. His next movie,* Kick-Ass, *will be released in 2009.*

Acknowledgements

My mum always told me to be polite and thank people if they do something for you. So many people have helped me in the preparation of this book I don't know where to start.

First, I must thank the people who made it possible to write this story – the variety acts, the stars, those who didn't make it to the top, those who did. Then I'd like to thank all those people who listened to my stories at dinner parties, and in conversation, and who nine times out of ten said: 'You should write a book.'

It took me years to put pen to paper. But with the encouragement of ALL my family, including my three super grandsons, one day I sat down and looked at a blank sheet of paper. I started to write – the result of which you will see in the pages that follow. Thanks to my wife Beryl, who reminded me of dates and stories long forgotten. To my daughter Yonnie (McInnes), features editor with the *Ayrshire Post*, who, in her (not very) spare time, took my efforts and made order out of chaos. To my son Chris, a film editor at STV, for his support (and intermittent nagging) and telling me to stop talking about it and finally get it started. To all my friends at the Post Office, the newsagents, the greengrocer boys, and all my *Cavalcade* 'boys' and 'girls' who still constantly stop me in the street for a few words in all parts of the country. To the charming Chinese family I met in a motorway café who smiled at me whilst talking away in their native tongue until I recognised the name 'Glen Michael' amongst all the chatter. Most of all, a very big thank you to my new friend and former Cavalcader, Mark Millar, who introduces this book with such kind words.

Lastly, to you, the reader, I hope you enjoy *Life's a Cavalcade*. It can be for you too. I thank you.

Glen Michael
August 2008

Prologue

'Thank you for watching . . . And goodbye.'

'CUE SIGNATURE TUNE. INTO CREDITS,' the autocue instructed. The studio was suddenly enveloped in blackness and the disembodied voice of the director boomed out of the studio speakers.

'Thanks, everyone,' he said. Then there was utter silence and a kind of deadness in the studio. Seconds before it had been full of sound, bright lights and all the people it takes to bring a TV production to life. It was December 1992 and I had just finished recording another edition of *Glen Michael's Cavalcade*.

As I picked up a few letters from my studio desk, a feeling of unease washed over me. I had been doing this same routine for years, but today was different. Week after week since April 1966 I was used to saying at the end of a recording: 'Take care . . . See you next week.' This time I was lying. How could I be OK? This was it. The goodbye. The last *Cavalcade*.

It had been arranged that I would be having a little going-away party. These are the sorts of occasions that I always dread attending. Everyone seems to laugh at nothing in particular, downing as much wine as they can before rushing off. The floor manager dug me in the ribs. I smiled at him and he said: 'Time to meet the big yins.' He turned on his heel and I followed.

The powers that be had asked me to let them know whom I would like

1

to invite to the party. I came up with a list of about two hundred, all those that I could remember who had worked on my show over the years – directors, lighting and sound engineers and countless others. Sound people in particular because I wanted to say sorry for the number of times I had given them stick when I had got everything right during a take, only to hear a voice saying: 'We didn't get that . . . Can we do it again?' Second time around was never the same; the first take is always the best, as Spencer Tracy used to say.

In the end, my guest list had been cut down to a select few – heads of departments and the like and, of course, my immediate family: my wife Beryl, daughter Yonnie and son Chris. Our programme controller, Gus (now Lord) Macdonald, met me in the plush mini-suite at the top of the STV buildings in Cowcaddens. The champagne corks were popped and very soon everyone was chatting away.

I started to glow, and as I looked around the room, everyone was in little groups talking away as if everything was quite normal. It wasn't, of course, at least not for me. After working for so many years on one of STV's most popular family programmes, I was out of a job and apprehensive about what the future held.

My thoughts were interrupted with the sound of a spoon tapping on a glass and silence fell as Gus Macdonald – the fifth programme controller I had worked with during my many years at STV – addressed the party, thanking me for all my time and work at the station.

'Nearly thirty years of *Cartoon Cavalcade*,' said Gus. I had a dreadful feeling I was going to get a gold watch. I was near to tears. Gus continued: 'Glen, it would seem you have played to over TWO BILLION viewers over that time. I don't think we will ever see the likes of that again in television. It's the end of an era.' The speech continued, glasses were topped up and raised, and a toast was proposed.

Later, after the party had ended, I found myself sitting alone in my chair in my dressing room, still in full make-up and wearing my colourful *Cavalcade* clothes. No watch, no cheque, just the immediate memory of some very nice people trying to make me feel good after my last TV appearance. So there I was, sipping at a nearly empty glass of champagne, trying in my mind's eye to create a picture of what the future might be. But all I saw were jumbled images of the past.

1

A West Country baby

How did it all start?

I would love to say I was born in a trunk on the side of a stage – but I wasn't. My father Arthur had itchy feet so we moved a lot. He was the black sheep of his family. I can picture him now, five foot nine, with iron-grey, wavy hair and a smile that could charm the birds from the trees. A born gambler, he was always looking for that elusive pot of gold.

As Dad moved around the country, so did his long-suffering wife Mabel – my mother – and Gerald, my older brother. In 1925 I was not yet a resident of this world, but I can picture the scene. Dad and Mum are in the lovely little seaside town of Paignton, Devon and he has mentioned to my mother that, once again, he has thoughts of moving on to pastures new. My mother does not respond with her usual 'All right, Artie,' but suggests that they stay put. She is pregnant with me, and even Dad – usually unfazed by anything – doesn't have an answer to that one.

I arrived at 6 a.m. on 16 May 1926, a bright and sunny morning, at 3 Roundham Cottages, The Cobb, Paignton. Arthur and Mabel Buckland now had another son, weighing in at six pounds and five ounces. To put a name to this bundle of joy was easy for my father: it had to be Cecil, after my father's brother who was killed flying over Oxford while training for service as a pilot in World War I.

I can't remember much about my schooldays. They are a bit of a blur, a hazy recollection of events that hardly add up to an education. We moved around so often that I found it hard to retain things, and I don't remember any teacher taking time to help me catch up. My father had been given a very good education, but sad to say he didn't use it to any great effect. He seemed to think that education didn't matter for me, and he himself had no thoughts towards the future: his philosophy of life was always to live for the moment. Life was a ball to him, and as a child I enjoyed it all as much as he did. But one day the ball would end . . . And then what? I don't remember leaving school. I don't remember one single teacher's name. And I was never in any one school enough to have any connection with other children.

So I recall almost nothing of my first school, but I do know that it was in the village of Countess Wear, just outside Exeter. I took a trip down memory lane some years ago to see if I could find it. To my great delight it was still there, although it had changed a bit since 1931. It is now a charming country cottage with roses around the main door. It still has railings outside – those, at least, I remember clearly, my mother holding me tightly by one hand as I trailed my little walking stick along the railings, making the sound of a train running along a railway track. My mother gently led me into the playground and a teacher came out and took over my hand from hers and led me into the tiny classroom. I cried and cried. Nothing changes. When I do my live Road Shows around primary schools I see that scene repeated over and over again and my heart goes out to the child and the mother. When I was let out to play on that first day I had only one thing on my mind: would my mum be there? She was, smiling and waving to give me confidence.

My father and mother had rented a wonderful, old-world thatched roof cottage for five shillings a week that stood in its own grounds overlooking the weir. Dad was employed as a car salesman in a showroom in Exeter and I can remember him telling me I was going to have a great sixth birthday. True to his word, on the day, a railway horse and cart rolled up to

the front of the cottage and the driver dragged off a huge wooden crate
about four feet long by two feet wide. With a cheery wave from the driver
the cart trundled away. Dad rushed off to get a hammer. Mum tore at the
cardboard, and I just got in the way. Excitement wasn't the word. I could
see a small hole at one side and made it bigger by inserting my finger and
pulling but only got a splinter for my trouble. I could see a wheel. I made
another hole to see part of something shiny and red. After more frantic
pawing at the cardboard, a small handle came into view. Dad was clattering
away with the hammer and soon we were knee-deep in wood shavings,
cardboard and paper. Mum said, 'Ah,' Dad said, 'Oh,' and I screamed, 'It's a
car! A pedal car!'

It was pillar-box red with real blow-up tyres, a hood that went up and
down and battery-operated headlights and sidelights. It was the best car I
had ever seen, and it was mine.

'Happy birthday,' said Dad. Mum gave me a big hug and I just stood
and looked at it. I found out later that it had cost £25 – a lot of money in
those days – and had come from Gammages of London. I had enormous
fun with that car. The only trouble was that no one in the village had seen
anything like it, and everyone wanted a ride. My brother Gerald even did
his nightly paper round in it, with me running alongside trying to get a
shot at driving. After all, it was mine!

A few months after my birthday Dad left his job at the car showroom
and we moved to Lyme Regis in Dorset. My car didn't go with us; it was
sold, as we needed the money. The idea was to open a boarding house and
take in paying guests. Lyme was a lovely little fishing village then, as it still
is today, and I often go back to savour the atmosphere. It brings back
memories of life in the little house we rented on the steep hill as you go
down to the harbour.

One of my pleasures was to go to the switchback room. The house had
huge cliffs at its back and over the years they had pushed onto the house.
The result was that one of the back bedrooms upstairs had a hump in the
middle of its shiny floor; I used to get a small rug and slide down it. The

guest house was a fair success . . . Mum cooked and looked after Gerald and I. Dad met the paying guests. Mum laid the tables and did the cleaning. Dad had guests to talk to. Mum made the beds and an old fisherman was given a few shillings to do the vegetables. Dad found other guests to entertain. Mum was the driving force and Dad was the image. Everyone liked him. He loved to sing and so did my mother. They would even sing at local concerts.

Dad always loved to sing in church and was a great churchgoer. As a young man in London his family were all at church morning and night, his father, and mother along with his two brothers and his sister. Dad used to sing as a baritone soloist in the choir and used to remind us of it at 6.30 a.m. every morning as he shaved while belting out 'Jerusalem'. He was delighted when the BBC choir, or rather, some members of it, started to become regulars at the guest house. They used to say it was a great place to relax away from the stresses of London so the weekends became musical magic for both Mum and Dad.

I had better explain a little about my father. What kind of man was Arthur Edward Buckland? Strange? Eccentric? Perhaps. But kind? Yes. In Lyme Regis in the 1930s life was hard for some people. Dad used to like a small glass of refreshment at the local pub at the bottom of the hill. He heard stories there about children going without a Christmas dinner and arranged for chickens to be left at the pub for the publican to ensure those deserving souls who needed Christmas cheer got it. On the other hand, when our family were a little short of money – even down to the last couple of pounds in my father's pockets – he would stick a pin in the runners and riders of the horse-racing page and head for the bookies. More often than not, his horse came in at the rear of the field of runners.

When he had the money, he used to buy cars second-hand from jockeys like Freddie Fox, who was as famous as Lester Piggott in those days. My first glimpse of Freddie was when I was a toddler. He was in full racing colours – there were no crash helmets in the 1930s, remember – walking away from me. His legs amazed me. He walked as if he was still on a horse with bandy legs that were the perfect shape to fit around the animal's body. I got used to being near racing people. Dad would take the car and tell Mum and me that we were going for a run. I remember Mum saying: 'Why is there such a crowd here?'

Dad would say: 'Oh, that'll be the race-goers heading for Sandown Park . . . And as we're nearly there, we might as well pop in.'

I don't know where the gambling fever came from, but it caused us a lot of trouble.

I loved living in Lyme Regis. We seemed to stay there longer than usual. I must have gone to the local school but don't recall anything about it. But I can remember playing with some of the children and, in particular, one day when Dad gave Gerald and I sixpence each to go to the cinema in the Marine Hall. Gerald and I dashed down the hill to the sea and onto the sands; you could walk along the sands to the cinema at the end of the prom. It was an afternoon showing and it started at 2 p.m. We had time to spare so we started to throw stones into the sea as we'd done many times before. Gerald was good at making a flat stone skim along the water. As I was looking for fresh stones to lob into the sea I noticed that Gerald had stopped throwing and was kneeling down. I rushed over to him. He put out his arms to stop me falling over.

I looked down at his feet and saw a seagull covered in thick, black oil. The poor bird was trying to get to its feet, only to slump back down again, fluttering its wings frantically as it did so. I looked at Gerald and I was sure he had a tear in his eye as he said: 'We must do something to help it.' The bird gave another flutter of its wings and a faint cry. Gerald suddenly said: 'Give me your money.'

I backed away.

'What for?' I said.

'Just give me your sixpence, Cecil,' his tone made it clear he wouldn't accept a refusal.

I searched in my trouser pocket and produced my only coin. He grabbed it and said: 'Wait here and don't move away from the bird.' With that he dashed away as fast as his legs would carry him. I watched as he ran along the sands and up onto the prom and out of sight. I sat down and waited and it seemed like hours as I waited for his return. But return he did, carrying a brown paper bag.

'What's that?' I said.

'Lard', came the terse reply. 'I got it from the butcher.

He sat down and started to rub the lard onto the bird, which tried to escape Gerald's greasy hands. A voice said: 'It's no use, you know.' I looked up to see an elderly man leaning on his walking stick. 'It's too far gone, I'm afraid', 'he said. 'Better put it out of its misery.' With that he pushed Gerald out of the way and swiftly brought his heavy walking stick crashing down on the bird's head. There was a little flutter of the wings, then all was still except for the sound of gentle crying. I felt like crying but it wasn't me . . . It was Gerald sitting with greasy hands still holding the little brown bag.

'Sorry, son,' said the man, walking away. It was the first time I had seen death and it was a shock. Gerald got to his feet and then knelt down on the damp sand. He started to dig with his bare hands until he had a fair-sized hollow. He lifted the now still bird and gently placed it into the hole. I started to push loose sand over the seagull until all we could see was a small mound in the sand. The sea was coming in and Gerald said: 'Let's go home.'

He took my hand and we must have looked a sorry pair as we walked back along the sands. When he got home Gerald told our story to Mum who gave us both a cuddle. It was an insight into my brother that I never forgot. He was indeed a gentle, kind lad.

We continued to have guests at our boarding house. One such customer was Brian Michie, who went on to produce a very famous stage show, *Youth Takes a Bow*. It would star a very young Morecambe and Wise – and more importantly, my future wife Beryl.

My time at Lyme Regis was coming to an end – although I didn't know it. Our family seemed to strike a bad patch and the guest house was not making money. My father broke his leg getting into the car outside the house and my brother and I got the measles.

I was laid up in my bedroom and told not to look out of the window into daylight. I did just that, of course, and to this day I still have a slightly red left eye. My brother was in another room and I could not understand why I wasn't being allowed to see him.

One day I was told that Gerald had been taken to the local hospital. His condition had deteriorated: not only did he have measles but he had developed mastoiditis. I was only seven years old and Gerald was coming up for thirteen years. The next thing I can remember was looking out of my window onto the front of the house and seeing four black horses with plumes standing in front of a hearse.

A small coffin was being placed into the hearse and as I gazed at the scene my mother came into my room. She was in tears. I asked: 'What's happening?' Mum sat on the bed and told me gently that Gerald had died.

'You are not well enough to go out,' said Mum, 'Old Joe will stay with you.' Joe was our vegetable-preparing fisherman.

I couldn't even go to Gerald's funeral.

So it was that my only brother was laid to rest high up on the hill overlooking Lyme Bay in a plot Dad got for the family. To this day there is only one name on it: Gerald Buckland – aged twelve years.

We left Lyme Regis and the next stage of our lives began. I think the loss of Gerald was a turning point for my mother and father. He became bitter and my mother withdrew into a shell. What was going to happen now? Once again my father came up with the move to end all moves. He had no job, and he had no savings – they had gone to the big bookies in the sky. So, he thought, if you can't beat them, why not join them? Time to enter domestic service. The Bucklands – Butler and Cook/ Housekeeper – are at your service. And what a service it would turn out to be.

2

On the move

REQUIRED

Married couple to work as butler and cook in titled household in the West Country. Only those with excellent references need apply.

I must confess that this advertisement is fictional. But it was typical of the sort of wanted ads for staff that you would find in many newspapers and magazines of the 1930s. There is one particular periodical still published today that has hardly changed in its call for domestic staff. It was from one such magazine that my father got his first job as a butler.

Of course, it was never going to be easy. The 'excellent references required' bit was the first stumbling block. He had no training as a butler. Certainly, his background was good – middle class – but that was all. Mum was in a better position having cooked in the boarding house at Lyme Regis. As a butler you were expected to be unobtrusive but immaculate, knowledgeable, and in control of any situation that might arise.

Let's take the last bit first. Dad could be relied upon to be in control of any situation. He had been flying by the seat of his pants for most of his life. What about the knowledgeable bit? Bang on target. What he didn't know he would make up. Unobtrusive and immaculate? Now that presented some difficulty. Dad had a loud voice and a heavy step. And as for being immaculate . . . Mum tried to see he had clean underwear and shirts but she could do nothing about the tomato-soup stains that sometimes appeared, on his jacket as if by magic, after his lunch. But my father was always optimistic so he set off with Mum and me for their first interview. He had seen the positions of cook and butler advertised and he was determined that we would be successful. On the other hand, he had no references, no real experience, and one great big problem . . . ME.

They had a child. In the 1930s, servants with children were not greeted with open arms. On arrival, I was pushed into the drawing room of a big country house ahead of Mum and Dad and told to sit down. I felt as if I was a dog about to be inspected before the transaction could be completed and money would change hands. I sat, and the interview started.

Dominating the room was a big, fat, ugly-looking man sitting in an armchair. He waved a chubby, accusatory finger in my direction.

'Is this yours?' he asked.

'Yes, sir, he's my son, Cecil,' replied my father. A lady, not as ugly as the man, was sitting in a nearby armchair. I tried to smile.

'You're the wife, are you?'

She was looking at my mother, who smiled back at her, while ignoring me completely.

'Yes,' she answered. The man shook his head, as if explaining simple arithmetic to a blankly obtuse classroom.

'We wanted a married couple. Don't want any more children, we've got two of our own, two dogs, and a nanny.'

He glanced in my direction and I sank deeper into my chair. The man continued.

'Where were you last employed and why did you leave? Were you sacked?'

My father laughed nervously. 'Oh dear, no. My wife and I ran a small hotel and we have decided to come into domestic service. My wife's cooking will amaze you.'

The man seemed unimpressed. He was looking at me again.

'No references, no experience, and you've got THAT!'

Waving absently in my direction, my father was quick with his answer.

'Don't worry about the boy. He'll be no trouble.'

The man stared into space for a while, nodded to himself and continued. 'Tell you what, I'll give you a three-month trial. If you're any good, you can stay, if not you're off. We have a cottage in the grounds that you can have and you can have the use of an old Austin 7 in the garage. You'll get your food and one day a week off. You start at 6 a.m., do the fires, and breakfast is 9 a.m. sharp. My morning papers must be ironed with no creases and Nanny gets her breakfast in the nursery along with the children. We have dinner parties most weekends. Sometimes for six or seven people. I can offer £10 a week for both of you.'

Once again, the chubby finger was pointed in my direction.

'But you must keep HIM out of our way. He can only eat in the kitchen.'

Well . . . How do you react, and what do you say, in such a situation? Dad rose to his feet and gave a deep bow to his future employer.

'I'm delighted to accept your offer.'

The man asked when my father and mother could start.

'Would tomorrow be alright?'

If my memory serves me right we were staying in a B & B at the time. The quicker we got out the less money we would have to pay. The lady of the house led us quite a walk down a tree-lined path to a cute cottage with two very small bedrooms and a small sitting room and kitchen. It smelled a bit musty but it would be home.

She left us at the gate and we waited for the country bus that would take us back to the nearest town, Dorchester, where we were staying. As I listened to Dad and Mum talking on the bus it came to light that we were going to be working for the chairman of a very well-known cheese company – one that is still going today.

After paying our bed-and-breakfast bill, five and sixpence for Mum and

Dad and half-price for me, we set off for our new home. All we had were two suitcases and not much money. Mum and Dad seemed to be OK at the new job. Mum was delighted to get into a kitchen again and everyone, including the frosty-faced Nanny, seemed to enjoy her chicken pies. Mum's fruit scones were also greeted with squeals of delight. Dad was thrilled with the Austin 7 and one of my strong memories of that time is of us pulling up at a country garage and Dad asking for a gallon of petrol. I can still see the man winding the wooden handle of the pump and Dad asking how much he had to pay. It was one and ninepence! Can you imagine the queues at a supermarket if that were the price now?

On their regular day off, Dad would pile us into the Austin 7 and off we would go to Dorchester. We would have tea at the same teashop each time and then go on to the picture house to see a film. It had to be the early showing because Dad didn't like driving in the dark. He was a very steady driver. So steady, in fact, that he never drove at more than 30 mph – ever.

For three hours we would enjoy the British Movietone News, a cartoon, a B picture (often a cowboy film), and the big feature film – all for 1s9d. We liked going to the pictures and we had a routine. It never varied. Dad always went for the back row, centre aisle. I was sent in first, Mum second, and Dad took the end seat on the aisle. He sat there because, as he said, if there was a fire – he could get out first. No matter what cinema we were in, he had to be in that seat or we simply didn't stay for the film. If the picture had started – in the dark – all you could hear above the soundtrack was my father shouting: 'Where's my seat? Mabel, where are you? Where's the boy? Usherette, where's your torch? For God's sake, Cecil, where are you? I can't see. Can you hear me? Can you hear me?'

A lone voice cried out during one particular performance, 'We can all bloody hear you!'

Yes, going to the pictures was never dull.

Being a butler seemed to be working out and my mother was always being praised for her cooking, but as time went on (and I'm talking about months, not years) I could see that Dad was getting bored. As for me, I must have gone to school, I suppose, but I don't remember it. Dad had a habit of forgetting to send me to school. We moved around so much that it was hard for the education authorities to pin us down, I suppose.

The inevitable work confrontation came one day when Dad had served breakfast and arranged the flowers in various pots around the house. As he came down the main staircase he saw one of his pots had been tipped onto his polished floor and there was water and flowers everywhere. Marching into the drawing room he confronted the boss to be told it had happened while Nanny was chasing the children. Dad demanded an apology from Nanny but was peremptorily told: 'Nonsense – clear it up.'

Nobody talked to my father like that. He marched out of the room and back to the kitchen where my mother was preparing lunch.

'That's the last straw, Mabel. That's the last time Nanny does that to me,' he said. 'We're leaving.'

I was eating some rather nice homemade soup and I promptly dropped the spoon into it, splashing my face with its hot contents. That soup was never finished as I was bundled away to the cottage with my mother still wiping her hands on her pinny and Dad leading the way at a pace that we couldn't keep up with. Bags were packed and, in a very short space of time, we were making for the bus. I remember Mum asking: 'What about our money – and their lunch?'

'To hell with the money – and their lunch,' was his reply.

We were heading for yet another bed and breakfast.

I would have been about ten years old at that time and I think our lifestyle was beginning to take its toll. I was becoming shy and quiet. If a knock came at the door I would try to hide under the table. If a stranger spoke to me I would start to stammer and go red in the face. And there was a bigger problem my trousers. I was a big lad for my age and I was beginning to feel embarrassed about wearing short pants. Dad would hear nothing of it.

'You'll wear short trousers until you're fourteen, like I did,' he said.

There were more tears from me, and a glowering look from my mother at Dad as she gave me a quick cuddle and a kiss on the cheek. 'Never mind, chicken,' she said. I never knew where that expression came from and it didn't make me feel any better. As I blew my nose on the hankie Mum had given me I felt, for the first time, the fluff on my upper lip. I had visions of me being the only boy in the world with short trousers AND a Clark Gable moustache. Maybe I could run away and join the circus? But the circus would have to wait because Dad must have had enough of the country life. The next stage of the Buckland's 'Grand Domestic Tour' took us to Tonbridge, Kent, and the home of a former lord mayor of London. I don't remember much about this stop-over apart from one glorious event.

One evening, there was a dinner party whose guests were all government ministers, MPs and their wives. Dad had everything organised and was polishing the glasses – something he was very good at. When he was finished they twinkled like the stars. Mum was in the kitchen preparing all the goodies and I sat patiently waiting for any leftovers. I was a growing lad. I loved my mum's roast potatoes and as the plates came back from the dining room I scanned the serving dishes full of roast beef and Yorkshire pudding with dark, thick gravy. I can still smell it now. My father suddenly crashed into the kitchen, laughing hysterically. Falling in a heap into the only chair in the room, he was red-faced with mirth.

Mum was very calm and asked: 'What's up, Artie?'

Dad was still laughing and said: 'You know that new Labour MP? The one who's getting all the publicity in the newspapers? He's just drunk the water out of the finger bowl. Flower petals and all.'

It wasn't long after that dinner party that Dad, once again, had words with his boss and we were on the road. This time we headed for the racing town of Newbury (Mum always suspected that the proximity of the racecourse was Dad's main reason for taking the job), and, according to Dad, we were going up in the world. Yes, wonder of wonders, Mum and

Dad were going to work for an earl. We took the bus from Victoria Station in London.

As I said, Dad never, ever, drove faster than 30 mph. He was always telling people that he had broken both his arms and legs in a car crash, hence his fear of high speeds. I don't know whether this tale was true or not. But while my father always watched his own speed, he had no control over other people. This was always going to be a problem if we used public transport. To get to our new job, we were on the long-distance bus heading out of London. I think it was a Green Line Coach and Dad had always liked them – until that day.

We reached open countryside and I was bored and sleepy, counting the cars that passed us and looking forward to seeing an AA patrolman on his motorcycle and sidecar. It was such a thrill to get a salute from them. We always sat on the back seat if we could as Dad, once again, thought that if anything was going to happen he could get out of the emergency door at the back. I don't think it ever crossed his mind that something just might hit us from behind. The coach was typical of the day: it held about forty people and was the driver unprotected from his passengers' attentions.

'What do you think you are doing?' my father's voice suddenly boomed. I had been dozing but was awake in an instant and knew his tone spelled trouble with a capital T. I thanked the Lord it wasn't me he was shouting at.

The driver was a portly man with a chubby face. Keeping his eye on the road, he told Dad: 'Sit down while I'm driving.' That was like a red rag to a bull.

Moving a step nearer to the driver, even though the motion of the bus made him unsteady on his feet, his voice boomed out again: 'Don't you know you're driving far too fast? You're going to kill us all if you're not careful.' I was sitting in one of the two front seats and could see the speedometer read 45 mph. As for killing all of us, there were only another two people besides us on the bus.

'Slow down,' insisted my father.

No response.

19

'Artie, come and sit down. Don't let the man upset you.' Mum was trying to defuse the situation. As far as I was concerned it was Dad who was upsetting the driver but Dad was beyond the point of no return.

'If you don't slow down I'll report you to your managing director who happens to be a personal friend of mine.' This was an old ploy he'd used many times. He'd seen his name on the side of the bus and remembered it. The other passengers didn't look as if they would be supporting Dad. Suddenly he yelled: 'Stop, I say . . . Right now! STOP!'

The driver did exactly as Dad had asked applying the brakes with full force and causing everyone to shoot forward in their seats. Except for my dear, demented Dad, who ended up sprawling on his backside on the bus stairs. The bus driver stood up. He wasn't so small after all. Looking down at Dad he said: 'What the bloody hell is up with you – are you off your head? I have to be in Newbury at a certain time and if I have to do 80 mph to be there I'll do it.'

Dad, struggling to his feet and trying to muster some dignity, said: 'Then you will do it without me and my family. Get our bags, Mabel, we're getting off this madman's bus.'

I was a little worried about the situation. It was getting dark outside and we were in the middle of open countryside. It was just like Laurel and Hardy. Yet *another* fine mess.

The driver placed our bags on the grass verge and Mum and I joined Dad by the side of the road. The driver looked at Mum and said: 'Sorry, madam.' He climbed into his bus, slammed it into gear, and was off. To add to our misery, as the bus disappeared out of sight, the driver put its interior lights on. They looked so welcoming in the gloom.

Dad picked up one suitcase and I tried to carry the other one with a little help from Mum. It was dark, silent, and beginning to feel cold. We must have looked a sorry sight, walking along with Mum in tears, Dad still exploding with anger and me trailing behind wondering what else could possibly happen.

3

Rubbing shoulders with the aristocracy

Our little adventure with, according to Dad, 'Donald Campbell at the wheel of a coach', had left us stranded in an unfamiliar wilderness. Mercifully, we only had to lug our suitcases a short distance through the growing gloom before a car stopped beside us. The kindly gentleman driver had spotted my mother and me; he didn't mention Dad. He offered us a lift and we were not slow to accept.

He was going to Newbury. Dad, with his usual cheek, asked him if he knew of a bed and breakfast that we could stay at and, as luck would have it, he did. Once again in my still-short life, I found myself sandwiched between my parents at dusk, with all our worldly belongings held in our hands, face to face with the lights of yet another B & B. But, compared with our predicament just a few hours before, the feeling of relief overwhelmed the melancholic sense of déjà vu. I can't tell you how well I slept that night.

The next day we made our way to Highclere Castle – home of the 6th Earl of Carnarvon – the country seat of the Herbert family and, it would appear, my home for the foreseeable future. All this was a surprise to me. But I was delighted to discover that I would be living in the largest mansion in Hampshire, with my parents holding the posts of butler and cook. Our living quarters had room for me – and it would seem without any fuss. I was welcome. Once again I have no memory of attending school. All I recall are vivid images of what happened at the castle.

I used to be allowed to wander the estate as I wished and what fun I had. There was a feeling of freedom and joy that I had never known before. What I didn't realise at the time was that this magnificent and extensive park had been designed by none other than Capability Brown between 1774 and 1777.

So who needed school? It was a boy's own paradise and I loved it. The earl himself was very pleasant to me and I used to do odd jobs around the castle. I had a feeling of belonging that I'd never experienced before. There were two families – those who lived above the stairs, and those who lived below the stairs. Literally 'Upstairs Downstairs', except in no way was my father a Hudson-type butler as portrayed in the television series. He was more like a polite Alf Garnett. He would grovel when it suited him but when he came downstairs, his complaints about the behaviour and manners of the so-called upper classes were the regular topics of conversation with Mum. She always said: 'We work with them, so we must respect them.'

It was the unwritten law in households of any note in those days for those who stayed the weekend to leave a tip of a few pounds on the guest dressing table on the day they were departing. My father always did that little bit extra for those he thought might be worth cultivating over their stay. 'Would you care for the daily paper, sir?' he would enquire with a practised smile. He would run small errands or bring an extra drink to their room as a nightcap. He was always very polite to the ladies. He was no fool and had a certain charm; I suspect many had a little 'thing' for him. He used to make them laugh and, without going too far, he could be accused of being a flirt. At least that's what I heard my mother say to him many a time, 'Artie, Artie, what will they think of you?'

I wonder what they did think.

But mostly I took little notice of life *in* the castle. What I really loved was getting out into the grounds. I'd find a branch that had fallen off a tree – one that was shaped like a bow – and dash in and out of the trees on the estate woodlands, pretending to shoot at the enemies of King Richard. I was, of course, Robin Hood. The only trouble was that my Merry Band had only one member. It all felt rather lonely, until one day when I was shouting: 'Stand still, you varlet, or I'll shoot.'

A voice said: 'Well done, sir!'

I had played so long on my own that the interruption came as a considerable shock. I saw a lad about my own age sitting in a toy car that instantly reminded me of the one that my father had got for me . . . And then sold.

The lad saw me staring at his small car and he said: 'Would you like a drive?' As I walked towards him he said: 'It's all electric, you know, no pedals, you just push this and away you go.'

With that he set off and swiftly drove in a circle around me.

'Here,' he said, 'you have a go.'

I didn't need a second invitation, I jumped into the car, and I was off. I did the same as my new friend sending the car in a circle round him, not once, but a few times. I think I would have been tempted to do even more if another voice saying, 'Well done, Robin', hadn't interrupted me. It made me jam the brake pedal down hard, which brought me to a violent stop that nearly threw me out of my seat. The sound of laughter was a relief – I had thought I might be getting into trouble for being so rough with the car. I climbed out and found the other voice belonged to another boy of about my age and size.

'My name's not Robin,' I said.

Laughing, he replied: 'I know that. We've seen you playing at outlaws a few times and we thought you must be Robin Hood. We always are.'

They both laughed again and the second boy said: 'Well, Robin, now you have a Merry Band. Let's change the game. From now on we're the Three Musketeers. One for all and all for one.'

For the rest of that afternoon we played and rode in the car and then played some more before I said that my parents would be wondering where I was. I waved my new friends farewell and ran back towards the castle. I had never felt so happy. I had friends – perhaps for the first time that I could remember.

During the time my parents were at the castle there were many days we played together with never a cross word between us. I found out their names were Freddie and Porky. It wasn't until after many weeks of playing that it all came to light. When I told Mum about my meetings with two boys in the woods she went pale and wanted to know who they were. I told her their names and she stared at me for a few moments.

'Are you sure the name was Porky?' she asked me.

I nodded, wondering what all this was leading up to. Without another word, Mum called Dad over.

'Have you heard this?' she said. 'Tell your father what you've just told me.'

Dad sat me down on a kitchen chair and asked me if I was making it up. 'You did say Porky?'

I nodded yes.

He sat back in his chair and sighing said, 'Well, you're certainly moving up in the world. Your new playmate is his lordship's eldest son, Lord Porchester, or Porky for short.'

The name Freddie meant nothing to them then but it did years later when Freddie became Fred Winter, champion jockey and world-famous racehorse trainer. Lord Porchester, I was delighted to see, became racing manager to the Queen many years later.

The time arrived when we left the employment of the earl and I think they must have had some problem getting another position because I found myself back at the bed and breakfast in the fair city of Dorchester. Of course, it was a place we now knew all too well. Dad had taken a job as a car salesman in a local garage which had a small showroom attached where they sold second-hand cars. They had a couple of mechanics and Dad was in charge. In fact, he was the only other employee.

One Saturday I was asked if I'd like to go with him to keep him company as he thought it wasn't going to be very busy. A typical kid, I was bored after half an hour. The only action was one of the mechanics continually bobbing into the small kitchen to make tea.

I got in and out of a couple of the cars, pretending to drive. I was about to get into my third car when the showroom doors opened and a couple came in followed by two children. Being shy, I made a swift exit to the kitchen. Peeping around the door, I saw a small-ish, middle-aged man and a smartly dressed lady with a boy and girl by her side. The man was talking to Dad and seemed interested in one of the cars. The lady was looking at another car with the boy. The girl caught my interest immediately. She was about my age and very pretty. Cars didn't seem to interest her much and she smiled at me. Things were looking up in Dorchester that Saturday afternoon.

Now, my parents were great theatregoers – mostly to the music hall of the day. Dad's stories about the stars are probably where my interest in the stage began. And I loved going to the pictures and seeing film stars. Little did I realise I was about to be introduced to one.

My name was called and I stepped into the centre of the showroom. Dad ushered the man towards me and I could sense that he wasn't really bothered about moving away from the car that he was inspecting. He had no choice as my father had a firm grip on his arm.

'Cecil, you'll never guess who this gentleman is.'

He was right – I was more interested in the girl. The man smiled at me and stretched out his hand saying: 'Hello, I'm Bobby Howes.'

Laughing, Dad explained: 'The great musical comedy and film star. Mr Howes is looking for a car.'

As I extended my sticky hand I felt a thrill go through me. I was shaking hands with a real star. He quickly dropped my hand and waved his own in the general direction of the boy and girl. Mr Howes mumbled a name that I missed, and then continued his introduction, ' . . . and my daughter Sally Ann.'

This name meant nothing to me until many years later when I saw her name in lights. Sally Ann Howes: star of stage and screen, including being the original Truly Scrumptious in the film *Chitty Chitty Bang Bang*. All I could see at that moment was this lovely girl smiling at me. I recall she had long, dark hair, a camel-hair coat with a belt tied in a knot, and long legs. I was in love with a dream. I didn't speak but grunted in a stupid, gormless way. Bobby bought the Standard 8 for £45 in cash and drove it away along with my dream girl, Sally Ann Howes, whom I never met again.

4

On the move again

In the 1930s, long before television, every home had a radio, be it large or small. It was the main entertainment in the household. We had a little Bakelite that worked by battery. The accumulator was a wonderful invention – but it always ran down just when you needed it the most.

That was usually on a Saturday night, when Dad and I would be huddled round the radio, listening to shows like John Sharman's *Music Hall*, a variety programme featuring all the big stars of the time. If we knew the accumulator was low I would be the one who would have to dash to Dad's garage and get them to put it on charge. Sometimes I would pick it up the following day, but if things were really urgent, they would have to lend me a replacement. Saturday night was bliss, with us laughing at comics like Stainless Stephens and singing along with musical stars like Anne Ziegler and Webster Booth. These were simple, but very happy, days.

And inevitably, just as I began to feel more settled than perhaps I ever had before, Dad's wanderlust stirred once again. I had seen various situations-vacant pages lying about so it was no shock when Dad announced: 'We're going to Corfe Castle tomorrow.' I looked at Mum who just looked back at me – a little wearily I thought. It wouldn't be a long drive, around twenty-odd miles, and it was another twenty miles from Swanage on the coast.

We set off in the morning on a fine day and were soon there. Our car, the one my father had borrowed from the garage along with a full tank of petrol, had been making funny noises and Dad was getting a bit worried about the return trip. As we drove into Corfe Castle the first thing I noticed was the local pub, and as we drove past the castle I made a mental note of what a good place it would be to play.

Dad had to stop to ask an old gent the way as we were looking for a Captain and Mrs Rodgers. He was leaning on his spade as if he was expecting this query and pointed to a large house a few hundred yards up the road. Dad crashed the gears noisily as we shot off at a fair rate (for him!) up a long drive and stopped at a large oak door. Two dogs, a Great Dane and a bulldog, were sitting outside it. Don't ask me why, but I didn't like the look of the place right from the start. The atmosphere was cold and unwelcoming.

My first impressions would turn out to be correct. By this time I was used to being interviewed . . . Well, not exactly interviewed. I had become used to sitting quietly in a corner while Mum and Dad answered questions and – if all went well – I was ignored. After a time I would drift off in a world of my own and dream of knights errant and damsels in distress.

'Cecil, your nose is running; wipe it,' Mum said, handing me a handkerchief as we stood on the front doorstep. 'Coughs and sneezes spread diseases. Use your handkerchief.'

She gave me a reassuring smile and a quick cuddle. A very thin girl of about twenty years of age answered the door.

Dad raised his trilby hat. 'My name is Buckland. We have an appointment with Captain Rodgers.'

Without a word, the girl stepped back into the house and we moved into a capacious hall with a stone floor. I jumped suddenly as something was licking my leg. It was the bulldog. Happy to join him was the Great Dane, who then began sniffing my crotch. I smacked it in an effort to ward it off and got a clip on the ear from my dad who told me to leave the dogs alone.

Soon we were in the presence of the captain and his wife. The dogs had retreated and the girl had shut the doors of the drawing room. I had recently seen a film with Basil Rathbone as Sherlock Holmes, and Nigel Bruce, as Dr Watson. I almost had to stifle a gasp – the captain, sitting in the best chair in the room, was a dead ringer for Dr Watson.

Apart from that initial moment of excitement, it was the usual boring routine. I sat in the corner, seen but not heard, while Mum and Dad sat on the settee facing the captain and his wife. And then questions, questions, questions. Before you could say 'the Hound of the Baskervilles' we were in the driveway and back in the car. Mum and Dad whispered together all the way back as I sat in the rear. She kept looking back at me and then at my father. The looks were odd.

Two days later we were back at Corfe Castle. This time we came by bus – the car had been returned and now we were going into domestic service with Captain and Mrs Rodgers.

We got off in the village. It was quite a walk to the big house on the hill with our two bags. There were few people about. The rain had started and the soles of my shoes were a bit thin and before long I could feel my feet getting wet. We arrived at the oak door and this time there were, thankfully, no dogs to greet us. Dad rang the bell and the same thin girl opened the door. I started to follow Mum and Dad into the hall when Dad turned, told me to wait for a moment, and the girl pushed me out onto the doorstep and slammed the door.

I was still wearing short trousers, standing in the rain with no coat or umbrella, on the front doorstep of a house that I didn't know. Just as I was starting to get really alarmed the front door opened and Dad came out, closing it behind him. 'Come on, son,' he said. He took my hand and we walked at a brisk pace back down the hill and a few hundred yards later crossed the road before arriving at a small cottage. It was near where we had asked the old man for directions the day of my parents' interview.

Dad knocked on the door and a man of around fifty answered it. 'Hello, it's Mr Buckland, isn't it?' he said. We were invited in and the man enquired: 'Is this the little chap?'

'Yes, his name's Cecil,' Dad informed him as he pushed me gently towards the glow of the small sitting room's oil lamp. A homely looking lady was sitting knitting.

'Come in, love, come in, my love,' she said, without getting up.

Dad looked at her.

'Thanks very much for helping us out,' he said.

Turning to the man, he continued, 'I'll talk to you tomorrow about the money.'

Dad took me by the hand.

'Be a good boy. I'll see you tomorrow.'

Suddenly, he was gone and I started to shake.

'Oh, you're cold, dear,' the lady said. 'Come on over to the fire and get warm.'

I wasn't cold but I was in shock and feeling that I'd been deserted. I was trying very hard to hold back the tears.

'It's the captain,' the man said. 'He won't have children up at the house so you'll be staying with us for a while. You'll be fine.'

'Didn't your father tell you?' asked the lady.

I shook my head in the negative.

'Come on, then,' she said as she got up from her comfy seat. 'A bowl of hot soup and a good night's sleep and you'll be as right as rain.'

I followed her into the small kitchen, sat down at the table, and was presented with her homemade soup and bread, which tasted very good. It had been a long time since breakfast. I felt a lot better after eating and the couple tried their best to make me feel welcome. I was gaining in confidence and when they said it was time for bed, I was ready.

The man wished me goodnight, the lady lit a candle, and we climbed the stairs. There were only two bedrooms, one to the left, and one to the right. She led me to the one on the right, which had a single bed in it, a wardrobe, one chair, and a small table. It was bitterly cold.

'The candle will heat the room up,' she said. 'And don't forget to blow it out before you go to sleep.' With that she was gone and the door was shut firmly.

Then silence.

I was eleven years old and in a strange place with no mother or father. I was so cold, had no nightclothes, and felt so sorry for myself that I silently cried myself to sleep.

Suddenly I was awake – wide-awake. I sat up in bed to see a young girl in her twenties with long dark hair standing at the end of my bed. She was holding a lit candle, my candle.

'Sorry,' did I waken you?' She smiled. 'Mum and Dad told me about you,' she continued in a rich Dorest tone. 'I'm a nurse and I got some time off from the hospital in Swanage. Thought I'd come home for the night and here you are in my bed. You're going to have to hutch up, my lad.'

With that she began to take her blouse off. I dived under the bedclothes and pulled them over my head. I could hear stifled laughter. The bed was up against the wall and if I could have made a hole in that wall I would have done. I pressed myself against it as hard as I could and then felt the mattress move and the heat of another body lying beside me.

A voice inquired: 'What's your name?'

I didn't answer. I couldn't answer.

Silence again. Then, 'Goodnight.'

That was the longest night of my life. I don't know if I slept or not. I must have done, I suppose, because daylight eventually arrived. I was the only one in the room. There was my candle on the bedside table as if nothing had happened. I found out later that my night nurse was called Judy. And I had been Punch . . . for one night only.

When I went downstairs I was greeted by the smell of bacon frying. A voice said. 'Morning, I heard you getting up and thought you might like some bacon and egg.' My nose took me into the kitchen. I was starving.

'Sit down, Cecil, and tuck in. You must be hungry.'

As I began to eat, she said: 'I'm Mrs Hart and my hubby's Bert. I think you met our daughter Judy last night, didn't you?'

I nodded in the affirmative as I had a mouthful of bacon. She made no mention of us being in the same bed. I wondered what was going to happen that night. I soon got my answer.

'She's off back to the hospital.'

I breathed a sigh of relief as I pushed another mouthful of crispy bacon into my already-full mouth.

'If you want to wash you can use the sink in the kitchen after you've eaten. We get the bath in from the shed for bath nights each Friday.'

I wondered if that included Judy.

Dad arrived just after I had finished eating. He had one of our suitcases with him. 'Here are your night things, clean shirts and socks. Your mother sorted them out for you,' he informed me. 'If you need anything else, let Mrs Hart know and we'll get it to you.'

It looked like I was going to be there for some time.

'Sorry about last night, son,' he apologised. 'Everything has been done in a bit of a rush.' He patted me on the head and turned his attention to Mrs Hart again. 'I'll pay you every week for Cecil's board and lodging, Mrs Hart.'

Dad was looking at me as if to say 'This is what we are going to do so don't fuss and take notice'.

'I've arranged for him to attend the local school. Our day off is Thursday.'

With that he made for the door – a quick wave to me and then he was gone.

Mrs Hart rushed to the open door and shouted, 'Don't worry, Mr Buckland, we'll look after him. He'll be one of the family.'

She was as good as her word. I was treated like one of the Hart family and I even got the bedroom to myself. Judy never intruded again. In fact, she treated me like a little brother.

School was another matter. The number of pupils was very small. I suppose there would be about thirty in the entire school, a blonde stone building. I can't remember what class I was in but I do remember the teacher, a tall, stooping, grey-haired man with a constant sniffle, putting me through tests and showing me up in front of the whole class: 'Don't you understand what I'm telling you? Nobody can be that stupid. God knows what you're going to do in life if you can't understand a simple sum like this. Go to the back of the class and I'll give you some chalk and a slate.'

To a backing track of giggles, I tried to explain that I had been to a great many schools during my family's travels – and often none at all. But it was no use. The head teacher knew my parents were domestics and not locals. We were outsiders; my teacher didn't help and the headmaster took his side. Their view: what was the point of trying to improve my education?

The trouble was, every school I had attended had a similar attitude. It was hopeless – a case of give him some paper and a pencil and let him doodle away his days here. He'll be moving on. If this happened today the social services would be called in.

I did make friends with some of the children. I think they felt sorry for me although they never said so. When we played football I always put my hand up to be the goalkeeper – that way I was always sure of a game. The Hart family tried to make a life of sorts for me. Mr Hart let me use his daughter's old bike and although it was a bit big for me, it was a ladies' one so I could jump off quickly if I got into any trouble. I used to love trying out tricks on it. This proved very useful in later life when I did my stage falls and film stunts. I recall one day going downhill with no hands on the handlebars and crashing right into some iron fencing with spikes on the top. My front wheel went between the two bars, the handlebars stopped the bike – and I sailed over the top, landing on an embankment in a heap. When I got up, I discovered my jacket had great tears right down the front – a testament to the sharpness of the spikes. That was one trick I never repeated.

Despite the peculiarity of my situation, looking back I think that perhaps my time at Corfe Castle was actually one of my better childhood experiences. There were still a lot of happy times with the family. I recall Mum and Dad wanting to have a 'refreshment' at the local pub in Corfe Castle one day. They had picked me up after school and we had been walking and talking. In those days children were not allowed into bars and, in any case, my mother would never be seen in a public house – even though she was partial to a port and lemon on occasions. At the entrance to the public bar was an alcove with bench seating on the right and left. Dad sat me down on the right and Mum took the left seat. It was quite cosy. There were no lights and it was getting quite dark. Dad went into the pub to get me some salted crisps and a port and lemon for Mum. As he opened the door the flash of light from within only served to make our alcove seem even darker. Suddenly, I was aware of a man coming into the alcove. We realised that he was completely unaware of our presence, as he let off the loudest and longest fart imaginable. It must have lasted all of six or seven seconds. He waited a moment, sighed, and said: 'Aaaahh. That's better.' Opening the door, still oblivious to us, he continued on his journey back to the well lit bar. There was a split second of silence and darkness, then first Mum, then I roared with uncontrollable laughter.

That situation was my first lesson in comedy – the element of surprise. In later years, when I came into showbiz as a comic, I summoned up that very same sound through a microphone to get laughs. Even today when I do my one-man show it still gets roars. People like dear old Harry Secombe called it a raspberry. That's the polite way of describing it . . .

5

Life at the Fairleys

I don't wish to linger on the subject, but the breaking of wind was one of the reasons why my family and Corfe Castle parted company. You may remember that the Rodgers had two dogs. One was fat and not unlike his owner in looks: a bulldog. The other was a sleek-looking Great Dane whose overwhelming joy in life seemed to be to nuzzle the crotch of anyone who happened to be within the sniffing area of its nose. I bore witness to the latter.

It was Dad's duty to serve afternoon tea at the stroke of 4 p.m. every day in the drawing room. It was always tea for two with toast (lightly done), scones and jam. He would enter to a roaring log fire, a very warm room and the two animals lying fast asleep by the hearth. Dad was placing his tray on the low coffee table – a manoeuvre that required him to bend at the waist. As he did so, the most dreadful odour was noticed by the captain, who lowered the paper he was reading to turn a baleful eye on his butler.

'Buckland! How dare you!'

To my father's eternal credit, he gave no reply but made a very quick exit. On reaching the safety of the kitchen Mum took one look at his flustered expression and enquired if everything was satisfactory with the tea.

'The tea's fine,' he said. 'It's that bloody bulldog again. And guess who got the blame as usual.'

The wind of change had blown through our lives once again . . . My parents did serve some sort of notice this time, however, and I recall a tearful farewell to the Hart family who had been very kind to me. We were even waved off by Mrs Rodgers. The captain was absent without leave. But the lady of the house, much to my amazement, stood on the front doorstep bidding us good luck. She even had a cuddle for my mother and a peck on the cheek for my father – which didn't go unnoticed. Dad said afterwards that he always got on well with Mrs Rodgers – say no more . . .

We set off down the long driveway of Corfe Castle in our newly acquired Austin 7, which Dad had picked up at a bargain price from a pig-farmer friend in the local pub. We got used to the smell over time . . .

All I knew about our next port of call was that it was in the middle of England and I was to stay in the main house again with Mum and Dad. I can't remember where it was or who the people were. I think they had something to do with the law and were retired. It was a large country house covered in ivy.

Dad was not long in getting his knickers in a twist there, though. Before we had even unpacked the order came from 'upstairs' to check the electricity. Dad's voice showed his deep concern.

'What are they talking about, Mabel?' he asked Mum.

She replied with a knowing smile. 'I think you'll find it has something to do with the generator you claimed you knew all about.'

Mum was always the one who fitted into a new place quickly – she had to. In those days it was not uncommon for big country houses to have their own generator in a building on the grounds. In this case it was housed in some kind of miniature mansion house – or maybe mausoleum is more accurate – covered in ivy and cobwebs. Inside was a very noisy-looking engine that ran on paraffin oil. The only way we knew that was because we found a tin of it on the floor. I put the oil in; Dad tried to work out how to start it up, but I found the button. We had electricity. I was delegated the task of doing this job when required and I got quite

36

good at it. In fact, I enjoyed the sense of power that it gave me, for once.

I can't remember the names of the people that Mum and Dad worked for there, but what I do recall is that they dressed for dinner every night. He always wore a dinner suit and she was in full-length eveningwear. I can see Mum now, sending Dad into the dining room with the first course, some rather nice home-made soup. They used to sit at a long table with the master at one end and the mistress at the other. That's what they wanted to be called – Master and Mistress. After they had finished the soup they would ring a small bell and Dad would then retrieve their empty plates, returning to the kitchen to collect the main course. It was often just one stuffed tomato on toast, sometimes mushrooms on toast, or scrambled egg on toast. In the kitchen we had roast chicken, fish or a chop. Mum always said we ate better than they did. I knew nothing about how the food bills looked at the end of the month and maybe that was one of the reasons we left there in a rather unusual manner.

Early one morning, around five o'clock, I was woken from a deep sleep, told to get dressed, and, without even time to wash, found myself outside in the dark, fed up and cold. The three of us were standing by our car, our two cases – holding all we had in the world – were already inside. I often wondered how we got everything into them. But there they were, sitting on the back seat, waiting for me to climb on top of one of them . . . as always.

'Push.'

Dad urged my mother and I to propel our small car on its way. As I placed my shoulder to the back of the car I wondered why he didn't just get in and start it up. The car started to roll down the gentle incline of the drive, the tyres crunching quietly on the gravel. Dad jumped into the driving seat as it gathered momentum, and it was left to Mum and me to keep pushing. By this time we were running at a fairly fast pace.

'Keep pushing, Cecil,' Mum said, and promptly jumped into the front seat, slamming the door behind her. Now, to my agile young mind, this created a problem. Although it was a four-seater there were only two doors. How was I going to get in?

Suddenly, I heard the motor start up and the car took off as if, it too, wanted to get away from my wet, sticky hands. The last push from me missed the back of the car and found fresh air. A screech of brakes and then Dad was at my side picking me up from the gravel drive.

'Don't play games,' he said. 'We have to get out of here.'

I was bundled into the back of the car via the driver's door and perched on top of one of the cases. Dad jumped in and crashed it into gear with a grinding sound that cut through the morning silence like a thousand angry dentist's drills. I had my hands over my ears as Mum said in a stage whisper that could be heard a mile away, 'Artie . . . the noise.'

The noise didn't seem to matter any more as Dad became drunk with power. His foot reached the floorboards as he strained for the dizzying speeds of 30 mph. Mum had a calming effect as she said: 'You can slow down now, Artie, we're out of sight of the big house.'

So what? Why were we driving along a deserted country road at five o'clock in the morning? Why did we have to push the car instead of starting it? Why? Why? Why? Dad supplied the answer to my silent thoughts.

'We did it, Mabel, we did it!' he said.

Did what? I wondered.

'That'll teach 'em to be rude to me,' he said.

'At eight o'clock the pair of them are going to get a shock. No breakfast, no tea, no warm toast, no morning papers. I can just see them sitting up in bed waiting and waiting and waiting. I'll bet they can't even boil an egg.'

Mum, ever the practical one, said, 'But, Artie, we never got paid.'

Laughing heartily he told Mum, 'Oh yes we did. I tapped him for our wages a week early and he coughed up.'

He started to sing, 'Bye Bye, Baby.' We stole into the early dawn to the sound of Dad singing and Mum crying. As for me, I was in the back thinking, oh no, not another B & B.

And there *was* another B & B. But not for long. Prompted by a distinct lack of funds, I was soon to be given a taste of life under the stars. My parents didn't have a reference to pass on to anyone who might want to employ them. So many walk-outs had left them without ready cash and no written praise for their undoubted, if always brief, good work. Artie had done it again.

He would probably keep doing it. The sequence of events that followed our escape from the big house remains a little hazy. I locked the good times in my memory and the bad times and everything in between I let go. But I won't forget finding myself in my Mum's arms on a moonlit night as we all lay together in a hedge by the side of a field. I was twelve years old and all this time later I can still feel the bitter cold.

My parents' solution – or perhaps their last resort – was taking me to a workhouse. I was put in a dormitory with countless men down on their luck. In the bed next to me was a young man of around thirty years old. I remember him being very serious and talking all the time. In broken English he told me he was a White Russian and he was waiting to be deported. He talked of war and how he hated the Germans. This was 1938 and another war was just around the corner. Perhaps he would have been classed as a terrorist today. He talked and talked to me as if he was speaking to a grown-up. I remember feeling frightened but, strangely, not of my friend in the next bed. I think he was only trying to be kind by chatting to me. It was the ten or so other beds and their occupants that made me feel so uneasy.

Their ages varied as much as their looks and went up to around seventy years old, I think. There was one who looked just like Fagin from *Oliver Twist* and many others that had the air of those recently released from prison. Not exactly the ideal place for a twelve-year-old child.

I had been separated from my parents by the workhouse rules of that time. What I couldn't understand was why my father wasn't in the dormitory with me. Was he even in the workhouse at all? Had something happened to him? And where was my mother?

I never found out. To this day it is a mystery. I like to think I was put there to be saved from another freezing night in the open air. I hope I'm right. Days blurred into each other in the workhouse. I can't say how long my stay might have been. But one morning I woke to be told that my parents were waiting to take me out.

I quickly collected what little possessions I had and left with a brief goodbye to my Russian friend. He looked sad at my departure. I often wonder what happened to him. At that time and in all the years that followed my parents never offered any explanation about when, how or why this had all happened. I simply accepted it and tried to blank it from my mind. The next thing I remember, I was in Eastbourne.

My parents took me to a pleasant, semi-detached house in a lovely area. We knocked on the door and a couple in their mid-forties opened it and invited us in. My first reaction was that this seemed to be a bit of a comedown from Highclere Castle. Perhaps I had become a bit of a snob. Dad said they had a lovely garden and that I should go and see it. I was taken down a long hall to a door that opened onto the garden at the back of the house.

I was glad I didn't have to listen to all the usual boring talk that would be going on inside. But after a while I was getting fed up with wandering around the garden. There was no adventure here. I glanced at the house, wondering when we would be ready to leave, and saw Mum and Dad and the couple looking at me through the window. Dad waved for me to come inside. I retraced my steps and was met in the hall by all four adults.

'Cecil,' began my father. 'Mr and Mrs Fairley would like you to come and stay with them for a while. Your mother and I have a job to go to in London and we can't take you, I'm afraid.'

'Please say yes,' said Mrs Fairley, smiling. 'We have no children of our own and we'd love to have you.'

I looked at Mum's face and I swear I saw a tear in her eye. But maybe it was a trick of the light. Dad ruffled my head fondly.

'We love you, son. You won't need anything in the way of clothes and things. Isn't that right, Mrs Fairley?'

'Oh yes,' she gushed. 'Your room's all ready.'

I felt a rush of blood to the head and a feeling of utter panic. Why did my father always drop bombshells like this without any warning? He never told me anything. My parents were heading for the door.

'See you soon,' said Mum. She rushed back to give me a crushing hug, taking all the breath out of my small frame. 'Don't worry,' she whispered.

Then they were gone.

Well, I thought, at least it's better than a B & B.

Mr and Mrs Fairley were as good as their word. I had a lovely little room. There were clothes for me and they fitted. I thought at the time that that was strange. How had they known my size? It was summer and so there was no mention of school. I was given regular meals at regular times. I was even taken to their church. It was High Church and I was tested for my voice. I was accepted for the choir and I liked it.

Mr Fairley was very kind to me but said very little. They had a car and I was taken on trips. I thought I could be happy with this life but I knew it would only be for a short while – or would it? It was at the Fairleys' in Eastbourne that I first got the theatre bug. It really started with my visits to the main bandstand on the esplanade. Every Sunday hundreds of people would grab a deckchair or vantage point to look down onto the esplanade itself. You could also avoid the regular collection that was made for the entertainment by being up there.

The lower section was where the posh people sat but from my position I could see everything by hanging over the rail. One of the attractions was the band of the Argyll and Sutherland Highlanders. What a sight they were, dressed in their colourful dress kilt outfits, their fluffy busbies blowing in the wind. And when they played their bagpipes, it was stirring enough to make you want to fight the devil himself.

They were very popular and they had solo musicians who were virtuosos. It seemed like they were from another world. This regular bandstand entertainment is something that you never see today, more's the pity. Another popular band was the Coldstream Guards. I remember they had a wonderful solo xylophone player who used to send the whole esplanade into raptures. When the band played something the people liked and knew, the applause was deafening. Almost at once, I realised I wanted some of that. I just wanted to be out there, bowing to all those people and hearing that clapping . . . I wanted them clapping for me. I didn't know how I was going to do it, but I decided there and then that do it I would.

What really sealed it was when the Fairleys took me to the Devonshire Park Theatre in Eastbourne to see a live summer show. They knew one of the singers and when they took me backstage to her dressing room I was in dreamland. We went behind the stage curtains and the first thing that hit me was the smell of greasepaint and carbolic soap. I was hooked. This was going to be my life.

Then I got a bit carried away.

One Saturday I was given money to go to the pictures. I opted for the Luxor Cinema, which happened to have a season of Cine-Variety. That meant you could see a main feature film, a newsreel, a B-picture, and maybe even a cartoon. However, my main reason for going was that the Billy Cotton Band was performing live on stage with Alan Breeze. I got my ticket and sat down right in the front so that I could see the artists as close up as possible.

The programme started at 1.30 p.m. and I was sitting there at 1 p.m. ready and waiting with a sense of excitement I had never felt before. I knew this was going to be special . . .

6

A family saga

The main film was *All Quiet on the Western Front* starring Lew Ayres. A war film to end all war films, it was made in 1930 and is now a recognised classic. In those days it wasn't easy for a boy of my age to get into such a film. I used the common trick: wait for a grown-up to go to the box office, ask them if I could come in with them and then give them my entrance money. Nine times out of ten the ploy worked.

The programme started on time. First came the adverts – the ideal time to try out the seat to see if it would go up and down. A sharp whisper from behind told me to sit still. I pulled a face and sat back down.

On came a cartoon. It was an old one that I had seen before. Next was the British Movietone newsreel then a Western featuring Gene Autry, the singing cowboy, with his wonder-horse, Champion. Along with millions of other kids of the 1930s and '40s, Gene was my hero. He kept the Wild West safe and never raised his hand in anger. At the slightest sign of trouble he would burst into song and everyone would be happy. The film was called *Git Along, Little Doggies*.

After the West had been won yet again, the lights went up. The deep-red velvet curtains closed over the huge silver screen where only a few moments before I had watched the five-foot-high face of my hero. I could see people's feet underneath the curtains and the sound of a trumpet tuning up softly. Suddenly, there was silence. I was so excited I could hardly sit still. A voice came over the loudspeaker.

'Ladies and gentlemen, the Luxor Cinema is delighted to present Billy Cotton and his all-star band.'

The curtains were drawn back to show the great man himself. A rotund figure even in those days, he hardly moved his arms to conduct as his signature tune, 'Somebody Stole My Gal', rang out. It was loud and it was brash. I loved it.

They put on the most wonderful band show – comedy numbers led by the entire band and romantic songs sung by Alan Breeze. He was called upon to do so many things in that wonderful show. The funny thing was that he had a very bad stutter when he talked. when he sang there wasn't a trace of his speech impediment.

Just as suddenly as it had started, it was all over. To the sounds of their signature tune – and, of course, thunderous applause from a half-filled cinema – the lights came up. As the curtains were drawn a feeling of loss washed over me instantly. I felt bereft. Ever since that day I have always enjoyed and felt a sense of elation at a live show. To watch one is great. But to be *in* one? That's even better.

Once again the lights dimmed and the curtains were drawn back to reveal the giant cinema screen. It was time for the big picture. *All Quiet on the Western Front* started. I have never liked violence of any sort – even today I have no time for dramas where blood and gore is the focus of the story. I much prefer a Hitchcockean approach that relies on the imagination of the audience. Whenever it got too much for me I'd make a visit to the toilet. I must have gone a dozen times or more during the running of the film. My mind was so taken up with the Billy Cotton Band Show that I couldn't concentrate on anything else. I hummed the tunes and giggled my way backwards and forwards up the aisles. On my last visit the picture had ended and I came out of the loo fighting against people who were leaving. I had no intention of following them. I made my way back to my empty seat and I waited as the people came in for the 4.30 p.m. show. I saw the Billy Cotton Band Show twice more that day.

It makes me laugh when I hear some of today's stage performers saying it's hard work doing one show every night. Billy's band did three shows in a day — eighteen shows a week — and maybe a Sunday concert. Their performances got better as I watched each show. The last one was the best.

I didn't wait for the last showing of *All Quiet on the Western Front*. It would have meant too many trips to the loo. As it was, I was starting to get some very funny looks from one of the usherettes. It was time to call it a day. When I got outside it was no longer daylight. As I made my way back to Mr and Mrs Fairley's house I wondered what they would say. When I arrived I was greeted (perhaps that's the wrong word) by not one, but two policemen. Mrs Fairley was in tears. Mr Fairley was just looking at me. His expression was not difficult to read.

'Where have you been?' said Mrs Fairley. 'You left here at mid-day.'

'Yes,' said Mr Fairley. 'We've been worried sick.'

His expression didn't match his words.

'Were you molested?' asked the older-looking policeman (more with hope in his voice than concern, I thought).

I took a deep breath. 'No. I was at the pictures,' was my faint reply.

Everyone replied incredulously with one voice.

'The PICTURES!?'

Mrs Fairley began to cry. Mr Fairley snorted down his nose and the two policemen put their hats on, turned on their heels, and left.

The following day Dad arrived. There was a behind-closed-doors meeting with Mr and Mrs Fairley and after a while Dad came up to my little bedroom and told me to pack a few things as we were leaving and I wouldn't be coming back. I never saw Mr and Mrs Fairley again. Dad seemed none too pleased and said nothing as I got into a car I hadn't seen before. As we drove off, I felt a little sad at not saying goodbye and more than a little worried about what was going on.

All the time I had been at Eastbourne I had only had letters from Mum hoping I was well. Nobody phoned in those days — that was only for the posh people. I had a feeling I'd been there on a kind of trial . . . But a trial for what? I never really did find out. As I got older I came to the conclusion that I had been put up for adoption. It was not uncommon in those days for people to come to a private arrangement. I had no feelings of anger at that. My parents must have found it very hard trying to keep their heads above water.

As we left Eastbourne behind us, Dad said we were going back to where they were working. My parents were no longer in London, and had now moved to Welwyn Garden City, just outside the capital. Mum and Dad were working for a spinster lady in a house on the outskirts of the town itself. I was given a room of my own and I did little jobs in the gardens.

It was 1939 and I was out of short trousers at last. My birthday had just come and gone and now I was a teenager: I was thirteen. I never attended another school.

Not long after I arrived at my latest home, I remember being called into the spinster lady's lounge along with Mum and Dad, the kitchen maid, plus the gardener and his wife. The radio was on and I can remember vividly the voice of Neville Chamberlain telling us we were at war. It was a lovely summer and it seemed so peaceful. After that, everywhere you went you saw the preparations for war. Yet, at first, nothing seemed to change at all.

Well, some things changed. My father for one. He was a very patriotic type of man and as he knew young men would be going to war he decided to change course. That included Mum and me. He always came up with a surprise, did 'my daddy'. I called him that when I was nervous of what he was going to do next. Surprise should have been his middle name. He got a job with a butcher's shop on the outskirts of Oxford. Again, he had no knowledge of the profession, but such trivial details would never stop my father. Driving the butcher's van, he did the deliveries. Not only that, he persuaded the owner to employ me.

By this time I was fourteen years old. He told the boss I was fifteen. I was set to work in the shop making sausages all day long. I had to thread a transparent tube of skin onto a machine. The machine then pumped the sausage meat into what became a long snake, which I then had to twist at intervals to make a sausage. When I wasn't doing that I was cleaning the butcher's blocks. They had to be stone white and they took some scrubbing with a wire brush. At the end of my first day I was exhausted.

Sometimes I was allowed to go out with Dad and help deliver. What they didn't know was that was the way I learned to drive. When we were out in the country Dad would say, 'Go on, have a go.'

That old van took some punishment. You could probably have heard me change gear in the centre of Oxford when I was still on the outskirts. Dad thought I should get a proper job so he got me an interview with a friend from his childhood days. It was at the factory of Morris Cowley in Oxford. The interview was short and sweet and before I knew it I was pulling a lever and turning out thousands and thousands of tiny washers. To my left was another boy doing exactly the same thing – only his washers were bigger than mine. I think he looked on me with pity.

After my first day Dad wanted to know how I had got on. I said I had done just fine, end of conversation. And also end of the job. I never went back. I had started on the Monday and on the Tuesday I left the house at 7.30 a.m. and set off for work . . . Or so they thought. Mum had made some sandwiches for me and a flask of tea. I got off the bus in Oxford and wondered how I was going to fill my day. I spotted a picture house and decided I would spend the afternoon there. Then I thought of the theatre, so I made my way to the Oxford Playhouse and looked at the photos of the actors and actresses outside. How I longed to have my photo up there.

I walked about the town for a few hours, ate my packed lunch, and paid for the cheapest seat to see an afternoon of magic in the cinema. At five o'clock I made my way home to be greeted by Dad and the same question: 'How did it go today?'

'Fine,' I said.

With an eager smile he added, 'Did you enjoy it?'

'Oh yes,' I said. 'Very much.'

More than he would ever know.

I repeated my actions of setting off for work every day and returning home complete with sandwiches and flask. Until the Friday. That was the day the sky fell in. I returned home and Mum was sitting with Dad at the kitchen table. Both were looking at me and not smiling. 'Did you enjoy today?' said Dad.

'Yes,' I replied. That was as far as I got.

'I'll bet you bloody well did – but *where* did you enjoy it? And where's your week's wages?'

I confessed all and told them how I felt. I was sorry, but I couldn't make washers all day. I wanted to do more with my life. I put on the tears. I'd seen film stars do it. In a flash, Mum was by my side and gave me a hug. Dad did the same after a while. The real problem was I had no money to add to our kitty, and we desperately needed it.

Things had to change again. At short notice – as usual – we headed for the windswept area of Westmorland. The adventure that was about to unfold took place at a little hamlet called Cliburn. Somehow my father had got the job as warden of an agriculture hostel that was home to Irish land workers. He was a kind of manager and Mum cooked for about twenty workers who lived in a dormitory and dined in the canteen. We had our own living quarters of a family room and two bedrooms. It was an all-wooden construction – hot in summer and cold in winter.

Mum adapted quickly and soon feeding so many mouths was easy for her. I had never seen a group of people eat so much in my life. They did very heavy work in the fields for long, long, hours and they were big lads. They loved Mum's style of cooking and Dad was always up for a laugh and they all loved that too.

It was a very happy little band at Cliburn – it even won some prize or other for being one of the best-run hostels in the country. We stayed there for some time before the call came for Dad and Mum to take over another hostel in a gorgeous little place called Lechlade near Cirencester in Gloucestershire.

It was the same set up and they did well, until one day two gentlemen in raincoats appeared asking for my father. A brief conversation was held behind closed doors and then, to my amazement, Dad left with them in a car. The whole hostel watched. My mother was in tears when she told me there had been some trouble and that we would have to go into Cirencester if we wanted to see Dad. The following day a man and a lady appeared at the hostel and Mum and I left. Mum booked into a B & B and later we found ourselves at the police station. We were allowed to see my father, who was not at all perturbed. He tried to explain.

It would seem he had left one of our long string of B & Bs some time ago without paying the bill. His offence was obtaining board and lodging by false pretences. In laymen's terms he was short of cash and I suppose panic took over and he walked away without paying. It cost him six months of his life, most of it spent in the prison library. Reading and writing were passions for him so he was in the right place. Mum and I visited him in Gloucester jail to be told, 'Keep your chins up.' He was sorry for all the trouble he had caused. I could see he had not only lost his liberty but his self-respect had vanished, and I suspect that was far more punishment for him than a few months at Her Majesty's pleasure.

My mother had to take on the role of breadwinner. Not an easy task, as she had been so used to Dad taking the reins and making decisions. Dad was always the dominant character of the two. But Mum was a delightful lady. Tall and slim, Mabel Eleanor Wilde, as her maiden name suggests, had an Irish background. She met Dad at their tennis club in Muswell Hill in London. I believe she was a very good doubles player. She played left-handed. There was a good reason for that, as her right arm was withered. It was the same length as a normal arm only it looked like a baby's. She had no strength in it but could use it with amazing dexterity. Mum could manipulate it so that she could hold a very heavy cooking pot close to her body with ease. When I was a baby I believe the doctor used to bring people to see me being bathed and all were amazed at how she managed.

Mum told me that when she was a baby her father was playing with her on the bed and she fell off, breaking her arm. It was never set correctly and the result was the withered arm. I suspect one of the reasons she married my father was the fact that he never ever mentioned her arm. He was always saying of her: 'Your mother's a brick.' In modern terms you can take that to mean 'I love her'. She in turn loved him for all his faults and failings. Her nature was to be kind, shy and gentle – the complete opposite of my father, who was bold and outgoing in conversation and action. I admired and loved him for that too.

I can remember when my mother was baking in a very large old-fashioned kitchen. I was in a high chair and there were pots on the old-fashioned cooker boiling away. She was at this large kitchen table with flour all over it and I can recall me flinging my arms about in excitement at the scene. I hit one of the pots with my arms and boiling water poured all over me. Quick as lightning Mum whipped me out of the chair and onto the flour-covered table. She started to roll me over and over, back and forth, back and forth, until I was covered in flour from head to toe. Evidently, the flour had acted as a seal. I was only grateful she didn't pop me into the oven to brown me off. But that was Mum . . . Children came first, no matter what. I loved her dearly.

So there we were: no father, no job, nowhere to live and no money. Mum had to find work so off we set by bus and by foot towards anywhere that might provide employment. She was a great walker. We called at hotels and restaurants to see if they wanted a cook or even a washer-up. I lost count of how many places we called at. Everywhere we went it was: 'Sorry, nothing I'm afraid.' I felt a bit of a fraud because there I was, fifteen years old and hanging on to my mother's apron strings. I was beginning to think I had to do something, and quick.

I can quite understand the funny looks we used to get as we called at hotels and eating places of all kinds. It must have been odd seeing a middle-aged woman with a teenager tagging along asking for any kind of work. I never said anything. Mum did all the talking and maybe that made it all seem stranger. We were both getting tired and feeling it was all a waste of time after a few days.

Then we had a breakthrough. Mum saw an advert in the local paper asking for a cook in a riverside hotel in a place called Bablock Hythe, near Oxford. She made an appointment for the following morning to go to the hotel to be interviewed. We got a bus and arrived at the riverside to find a ferry that held about three cars. On the opposite riverbank stood a small hotel. We crossed on the ferry, made ourselves known at reception, and were greeted by a very pleasant man who introduced his wife. They were the owners; they sat us down and Mum talked of how she had been in service and so on. They looked at me and asked if her husband was with her. At this Mum broke down in tears. These people were so kind. They brought tea and scones for us and tried to make Mum feel a bit better.

Mum told them about Dad and our problems. In no time at all it was all over. It was agreed Mum would be their cook and she could start immediately. They even said I could work there. The ferry belonged to them and they said I could work it along with another local lad. They could give us a two-bedroomed wooden chalet on the other side of the river as they used to let chalets out to holidaymakers during the summer. They would take a pound a week for the chalet. We were overjoyed as we came out and crossed on the ferry to catch our bus. The next day we left our B & B. How carefully Mum paid the bill, insisting on a receipt that said – 'Paid in Full'.

We only had one suitcase now. As we arrived at our new home we both found it strange that we didn't have Dad to tell us what to do. The 'Little Wooden Hut' – as I named it – made a cosy home. It had a log-burning stove in the middle of the living room, two small bedrooms and a tiny bathroom.

We had been given the keys and Mum was told to settle in and report to start cooking breakfasts at 6 a.m. the following morning. No mention of my job at the ferry. I started to unpack the few odd things I had from our single suitcase and noticed Mum having a little weep. I never let her know I had seen her crying.

51

The following morning Mum was up bright and early. I decided I would go with her. We had to call the ferry as it was on the other side of the river. A young lad about my age was pulling it over.

'We don't start until six,' he said, as we climbed aboard.

Mum explained she would be working at the hotel and he said: 'Don't know how that's going to work then.'

From the ferry we walked into the hotel, as the main doors were already open. The boss showed Mum the kitchen and left her to it. There were only a few guests and Mum was happy in the kitchen. I tried to help with all the little things she found for me to do. The hotel guests got their food on time and one even left some folding money under his plate. It was all very much a one-man band but she seemed to enjoy it.

The boss came in as we were washing up and told Mum that she'd been a roaring success. He asked if she was happy and the smile on her face said it all. I can't begin to explain the relief and contentment both Mum and I felt after all that had happened in the previous few months. Over the next couple of days I did my bit in the kitchen and odd jobs about the hotel. Then the boss came to me when I was carrying coal into the hotel lounge and asked if I could drive. I thought about the butcher's van . . . I didn't think it was a good idea to tell him that story. But some form of the truth would be best.

'I can drive but I'm not seventeen yet,' I told him.

'No,' he said with a twinkle in his eye. 'But you can drive on private property.' I agreed, the twinkle in my eye this time. He then took me outside and showed me a car. I think it was a Vauxhall.

'This is a private car park. Feel free to practise in your spare time. You could be useful in the busy season to run errands for us when you get a licence.

'Just ask for the keys,' was his parting shot as he walked away.

I took advantage of his offer and every spare moment I was round and round that car park until I could truly say I could drive. He also came up with the offer of my main job. The boy that pulled the ferry needed another person to share the load during the summer months when it was busy. The idea was that I would work the morning shift and hold the ferry on the Little Wooden Hut side of the riverbank. Then I could ferry Mum over in time to start breakfast. I would continue to transport cars and passengers back and forth until lunchtime when the other boy would take over. For this I would be paid a salary. I worked seven days – Sunday was the busiest day – and I was paid the princely sum of £3.

I was a millionaire.

The ferry was a flat-bottomed barge with flaps that dropped down both sides so cars could get off on either bank. We carried a maximum of three cars and as many foot passengers as could get on. I had to stand on the ferry on the left-hand side where a huge wire ran through two rollers, one each at either end. With one foot on the ferry I would pull on the wire that was attached to both sides of the riverbank. When you had three cars and about twenty foot passengers it was tough going. Sometimes it would get stuck on landing and to get it off required the help of a long pole and sometimes a passenger or two as well.

Many a time I had to make a quick jump to avoid a captainless ship sailing without me. In summer we had many visitors and so to augment my salary I would resort to 'mugging' for tips. A smile to a passenger would sometimes result in a sixpence or two. If it happened I would grin from ear to ear in the hope that more fortune would come my way.

Sometimes it backfired and I would get: 'What the bloody hell are you grinning at.' Many of my passengers were regulars and most used to like to pass the time of day with me. There was one in particular who used to come down on a regular basis. He had a boat on the river and used to dine on Mum's food at the hotel. At weekends he always had a couple of young men with him. I noticed I never saw the same one twice.

One day he came over to me when I was trying to get the ferry off the bank with my trusty pole. 'May I help?' he asked.

'No thanks,' I replied as I made my Superman leap aboard my ship. When we were under sail he came over to me at the wire as I was pulling with all my strength to keep us moving. 'Are you always going to do this?' he enquired.

To this day, I don't know why I said: 'Oh no, I'm thinking of going to London soon.'

'Good for you.'

He slipped a one-pound note into my hand and, giving it a little squeeze, said, 'If you do go to London, look me up.' He reached into his bright yellow waistcoat pocket and produced a small visiting card. I made a very good cricketing slip catch as he flicked it towards me. Then we grounded.

When all my cars and passengers had left my floating motorway, I dared to look at the card. It belonged to the editor of a well-known Sunday newspaper. He later became a knight. I did eventually go to London but I never looked him up. But it was his casual remark that set me on that first step towards a life in show business.

The year was 1943. My seventeenth birthday had come and gone and I was legally old enough to go on the open road under my own steam. I became quite friendly with the young lad Joe who was my ferry partner. We used to talk of what we would like to do with our lives. I suppose dreams would be a better way of putting it. He talked of the day he would drive a bus. I made him laugh by saying I was going to Hollywood to be a film star. He would shout out when passengers were on the ferry: 'Come on, Bogie – Hollywood or bust,' and start the ferry up. Everyone would smile and titter.

It was about the end of May 1943 that I made a move. I had finished my morning stint, had a turn at driving the car, completed a few odd jobs at the hotel and waited for Mum. I took her on the ferry back to our Little Wooden Hut. We had some cooked tea that she had saved from the hotel. I put the radio on and we sat together. Mum was reading. I switched the radio off and the silence made her put her paper down. It's now or never, I thought.

'Mum,' I said. 'Can we talk?' I had been thinking about it for days. As I pulled the ferry backwards and forwards over the river I had rehearsed all the different ways of telling Mum what I wanted to do.

I wanted to go away.

Mum sat and listened as I tried in a bumbling way to explain how I wanted to go to the big city – to London. She hardly said a word against my going. It meant I had to leave her on her own and that made me feel as if I was deserting her. Mum told me that she was all right at the hotel and that she could look after herself. That made me feel even worse, of course. Then she, in her usual way, solved the whole thing. She said she wouldn't stand in my way if I promised to come back to her if I found life was not what I hoped it would be. Her final words were: 'Your father and I know you have had a hard time being taken here, there, and everywhere, but it's just something we had to do. It was all we could do to keep you with us sometimes. Go, but keep in touch . . . please.'

By this time she was near to tears and I was trying hard not to show my feelings. The next day I talked to the boss at the hotel and told him I wanted to leave. He was very understanding and said that my mother would always have a job and a home there. My idea was to try and send money back to her – but first I had to earn some. A week later, a Monday, I packed a small overnight bag given to me by the boss. As I stood waiting for the ferry to take me on the first leg of the journey, Mum came out of the hotel, hugged me, and slipped some money into my hand. It was four crisp pound notes and a ten-shilling note.

'I'm sorry it can't be more,' she said.

At that moment I nearly changed my mind about going. I felt as if I was walking away from a mother I loved and taking money she needed – as well as going into the unknown world. I could stay and be safe or go and maybe fail. As these thoughts raced through my mind the situation was resolved for me.

Mum was smiling at me.

'Go,' she said. 'You can always come back. I'll always be here.' That did it. I jumped onto the ferry and Joe started it off. I was the only one on it.

No cars. No passengers. It seemed symbolic in a way. I felt like John Wayne in the last scene of a film. I could almost hear the music swelling up as I waved at Mum on the riverbank. Joe landed the ferry safely as usual and I stepped onto dry land.

'Bye, Joe,' I cried.

Joe just gave a wave and shouted, 'I wish I was going.'

I tripped as I turned, caught my hand on the ferry wire and it drew blood. A little piece of me left behind, I thought. Then I was off on the road to fame and fortune. That was the dream. I just hoped it wouldn't turn into a nightmare.

7

The lure of London

I had about £10 of my own plus Mum's £4 10 shillings. After paying my fare to London, I sat on the train and counted my money. What would I do? Where would I live? How would I get into show business?

I did have a plan of sorts. Ever since I had been in Eastbourne and seen the Billy Cotton Band Show, I had developed this performing bug. Going to the cinema only added to it. I used to go to my bedroom and stand in front of my wardrobe mirror and act out scenes I had remembered. I would copy the accents of various stars and pretend to be Edward G. Robinson or James Stewart. I was also a great fan of radio variety shows and stars like Robb Wilton. I had written a seven-minute act with gags I'd picked up from radio comics or stories I had heard in all sorts of places. And I had one great finish to my act – Winston Churchill. I could mimic his voice perfectly. In those days, you had to have a finish. Young stand-up comics of today just do a string of patter and then say, 'Thank you very much . . . and goodnight.' But in the forties, if you didn't have a song or a dance routine to end your act, you were a dead duck. No agent would look at you and the audience would certainly not give you their kind applause. Although on the train to London, I knew none of this.

I arrived with my small bag and stood on the platform as if waiting for something to happen. I gave myself a shake and made my way out of one of the many exits. A line of taxicabs was waiting. A scene I had watched a hundred times in films was of the star coming out of Grand Central Station, New York, and climbing into a taxi. I had never done anything like that in real life. Now was the time to do it. I had money in my pocket. I could be the star.

'Taxi!' I called out. Up rolled a big black London cab. The driver had a round red face with droopy eyes.

'Where to, sonny?' he snapped.

'I . . . er . . . er . . . ' I stuttered as I opened the door of the cab and promptly fell in a heap on the floor. I looked up to see him watching me in his mirror.

'Do you want a hotel?' he asked.

'Er . . . er . . . yes,' I said without thinking of what I was saying.

'Right,' he said, reaching out of his window with one arm and slammed my door shut. 'The Strand Palace do you?'

I made no reply as he shot off at speed with me trying to keep hold of my small case, packed with a change of shirt, socks, a bar of soap and one small towel. As we drove I couldn't take my eyes off the traffic, the people thronging the pavements, and the buildings. In far too short a time we pulled up. A hand reached out to open my door.

'Two and six, son,' the driver said as I climbed out.

I fumbled in my pocket and took out my change, carefully counting out two shillings and six single pennies. While I was doing this, I could feel his eyes on me. I placed my money in his outstretched hand. He took it and paused a moment.

'You just come up from the country?' he asked.

I nodded feeling the blood rushing to my cheeks. He nodded as if to say, 'I thought so'.

'A word of advice, son,' he said in a more gentle voice. 'When you get a cab you always give a tip. Always.' I reached into my trouser pocket only to be halted.

'No, no. Next time.'

He smiled and once again slammed the cab into gear.

'Good luck, son,' he shouted above the sound of the engine as he did a U-turn to go back the way we had come.

I turned and looked at my impressive new home. I walked inside and up to the reception desk. On the counter was a small card telling me the Strand Palace could offer accommodation for 12s 6d a night, bed and breakfast. I signed in, was given a key, and found my room on the second floor. It was small with a tiny bathroom. To me it was the most luxurious suite in the world and I was Cary Grant.

That night I walked all over the West End until after midnight. Back at the hotel, after all the excitement, I realised I was very hungry. I would have to wait until breakfast and I went to sleep dreaming of what I would eat come the morning.

At 7:30 a.m. on the dot I walked into the dining room and sat down. I was the only one there. After a while the doors of the service entrance opened and a waiter appeared. 'Follow me, sir,'

He arrived at my table.

'I already have a table,' I told him.

'Yes, sir,' he said with utter disdain. 'But that is a table for six.'

I meekly followed him to a table for two, tucked up in a corner of the room. I had made up my mind to eat them out of house and home and order everything that was going. I started with coffee. I ordered a pot and drank that right away, got another, this time along with a rack of toast. Then I ordered porridge and two eggs and bacon along with more toast and more coffee. By this time the little table for two in the corner was attracting the attention of many of the other waiters – so much so that a portly, tail-suited one, who I took to be the head waiter, came over to me.

'Will SIR,' he emphasised the 'sir', obviously seeing I was very young. 'Will sir,' he continued, 'be lunching with us?'

'Er . . . no,' I said.

'Thank you, sir,' he replied.

He did a half-bow and, as he walked away, I heard him say to one of his colleagues as they passed. 'Snotty-nosed kid. Too much money.'

Rather than being insulted I was really quite pleased I'd made such an impression on one so used to seeing wealthy people. Maybe my act would go well when I got the chance to do it.

By 9 a.m. I was walking up Charing Cross Road. I knew from everything I had read in newspapers and books like *The Performer* that this was the place to find an agent. Get an agent and you might get a job. In the 1940s all the agents you would ever want had offices in Charing Cross Road. You would have to climb maybe three flights of stairs to an office to be told by some snooty outer-office girl that the agent 'wasn't in', or to 'come back tomorrow'. A good one was, 'he's in Hollywood doing deals.' That meant he had nothing to do and was probably having a coffee in the Express Dairy.

I found the Express Dairy by chance. I needed a drink after suffering around two hours of repeated no's everywhere I called. I walked down Charing Cross Road and saw people milling around what I thought was a shop window. When I got closer I saw the Express Dairy sign. Once inside I got the shock of my young life. It was brimfull of people sitting, standing or walking about from table to table, and laughter filled the air along with the clink of coffee cups and the smell of cigarette and cigar smoke. All in all, it was a hive of activity.

Finding a free seat wasn't easy. I saw a table where three people were sitting and the fourth chair was vacant. In the bustle of London, I decided that must represent an opportunity.

I took a deep breath and moved to take the space and sit down. As soon as my hand touched the chair the conversation stopped. Three stony faces looked up at me. It was plainly obvious that I was not welcome so I gently removed my hand and slid away like a man who'd been caught with his fingers in the till.

I saw a table for two was now vacant right at the back of the café so I made for it as fast as I could and sat down. I looked around in wonderment. The room was as colourful as Aladdin's cave, with myriad faces and outfits. Some wore suits, jumpers, shirts, some had long hair, some no hair, some were smiling and some were deep in conversation. There was much laughter and a few long faces. It was a world of its own and I became fascinated with the bustle as people came in and out of the room, stopping at one table for a moment, then moving on to another.

I was completely unaware of a young man standing beside me. I jumped when a voice said: 'Mind if I sit here?'

A smile broke out on his tanned face. I stared at him. Tanned? He must have been abroad.

He sat down.

'Have you had something?' he enquired.

'Er, no, no,' I stammered.

'Coffee?' I nodded in the affirmative.

'Two coffees, Nancy,' he said as he slapped his knee and tickled the waitress who happened to be gathering cups on the next table. 'Coming right up, Bob,' she blushed as she scampered away.

He turned his attention back to me.

'You new to London?'

'You could say that,' I replied, still staring wide-eyed at his tanned face. He laughed.

'Don't worry – I'm not a poof.' I nearly died. It had never entered my mind.

'I've just been doing an audition for old Manny Jay and a bit of slap makes you look better,' he said. It was my first lesson in theatre language – slap meant make-up. 'I have to go back in fifteen minutes to see if I got the job,' he grinned.

'Got what?' I asked.

'A spot in *Nudes on Parade*', he replied. 'It's going up north in a couple of weeks . . . Opens at Attercliffe Palace.'

'Where's that?' I said.

'My God . . . You are new to London,' he laughed.

The pleasant-faced waitress arrived with our two coffees. She giggled as my new friend produced a ten-shilling note as payment. 'Ta' she said.

'Change, change, quick, quick,' he called after her. He leaned in towards me as if he was going to tell me something in confidence. By now I was living in fear of making a complete fool of myself in the eyes of my new-found companion.

'I'm a light comic,' he said with great pride. Then out of the blue he asked, 'What do you do?'

'Me?' I said, playing for time. 'Er . . . me . . . I'm a drummer comedian.' I liked Gene Krupa, the famous American drummer, and I used to pretend to play the drums with a couple of drumsticks that one of the hotel entertainers had left behind at Bablock Hythe.

'Oh, you're a comic,' said my theatrical friend with a tone of respect.

'Yes,' I replied.

'Would you like another coffee?' I asked, trying to change the subject.

'No thanks, I'm going to chase my change up – I need the money. Bye!'

And then he was gone. I finished my coffee and left. But I would return to the Express Dairy time and time again.

Every morning I would break off climbing the stairs to agents' offices and enjoy a black coffee with a little hot milk. Maybe even a second one if I had the time. It's a habit I have to this day, over sixty years on. It's the only drug I have ever taken.

Over time I got to know the running of that Express Dairy. It was the agreed meeting place of all the pros (professional theatrical artists) that were either in or out of work. If you were in work, you came to brag about it. If you were out of work, you came to try and hear a little bit of information that might lead to you getting a job.

People were very wary if your face wasn't known and you sat at a table uninvited. At any given time you could see stars like Max Miller – the 'Cheeky Chappie' of his day. He always finished his act with a song like 'Be Sincere in Everything You Do'. It would bring tears of emotion to your eyes when a few moments before there would have been tears of laughter.

Max always had the best table for service and rarely paid for anything.

He would hold court and his table would have other stars at it like Max Wall, Tommy Trinder and Donald Peers. At other tables you would find the also-rans: the number-two comics and acts telling their tales of when they knocked them dead last week at the Empire, West Hartlepool, or the Tivoli, New Brighton. Mostly the stories were exaggerated but they were told not as lies, but as dreams. If they were not exactly true, then one day they might be.

There would be dancers looking for any information on auditions for new shows that were going on tour. Some would be sipping coffee while they waited for word to see if they had made it into a show. They were all in the same boat so there were no tears or tantrums. There was comradeship amongst the wolves in this little corner of show business.

In my efforts to find work I must have walked miles and miles. Being young I never thought about it at the time but now I break out in a cold sweat when I recall all the unforgiving stone stairs that I climbed.

I remember an encounter with an agent I found in a back street off Piccadilly. He had an office behind a rehearsal room. You came in off the street, walked through the rehearsal room and up a flight of very narrow stairs, at the top of which was a black door. I knocked and a voice commanded me to come in. As I opened the door it hit the desk. And behind the desk was a stocky little man who looked just like Danny DeVito. He had to lean forwards towards me or he would have hit his head on the curved roof of the eaves. I had to stoop as I tried to get in and close the door behind me.

'Do you have an appointment?' he asked, glancing down at a solitary piece of paper on his desk.

'I just came up on the chance that you might be doing a show and needed an artist,' I replied.

'Do you have a girl in your act?' he leered. I said I didn't and he looked very disappointed.

'I need nudes and they all seem to be working,' he said. 'Shut the door as you go out and mind the handle – it sometimes comes off.'

He returned to scrutinising the sheet of paper he was drawing on. As I shut the door the handle did come off, sure enough. I muttered, 'Bastard' leaving it lying where it had dropped. I retraced my steps through the dirty-looking rehearsal room and into the sunlit street, suddenly feeling very lonely. I had been in London for only four days and it felt like four months. My plans weren't working out. Money was getting short. I would have to do something.

The one thing I did notice about my new life in London was the people. There were so many of them. On one occasion I was feeling a bit low and in need of some company. I am not a religious man and don't go to church as often as I should, but I found my wandering had taken me more by chance than design towards St Paul's Cathedral in the City. The last time I had been there was with my parents.

I was walking down Ludgate Hill after I had made my round of the agents to no avail as usual. Without warning, I found myself moving against a tide of people. Everyone was going the opposite way to me. I was getting pushed, jostled, and banged, as I tried to go downhill. I began to panic and stood still as people rushed by, seemingly going faster and faster. Nobody looked at me and nobody stopped. I put my head forward to start walking again and as I did so I saw something flutter down to the pavement. It was a brown ten-shilling note. I put my foot out and tried to cover it but I missed. I tried again, thinking everyone was surely watching me. This time I got it. I left my foot over it and looked up expecting someone to stop and jeer at me for stealing the ten-shilling note. I was wrong. People kept on walking and I bent down, picked it up, and held it in my sweaty hand.

I walked as fast as my legs would carry me until I found a side street that was quiet. I looked at my find. Sure enough, it was ten shillings. I hoped the person who dropped it didn't need it. It would certainly buy me a few meals. I never found out where all those people were going and I never did make it to St Paul's. I had fish and chips instead.

My trips to the Express Dairy were becoming more frequent. I was getting short of money and time, all the while despairing that I would never get a chance to even show what I could do to an agent. I was having my coffee with its splash of hot milk when I heard the next table greet a young lady with: 'Darling, where have you been, my sweet?'

She flung her arms wide and nearly knocked my coffee out of my hand just as I was about to taste it for heat.

'I've been doing my six weeks, darling,' she said.

I laughed out loud thinking she must have been in jail. I had seen prostitutes all over the West End in my wanderings and found many of them very pleasant to chat with. Some could be funny and very kind, depending on how you talked to them.

'Did I say something funny?'

It was the young lady talking directly to me.

'Sorry,' I said. 'I was just thinking it must be hard doing six weeks in a place like that.'

'A place like WHAT?' she asked, staring hard at me with anger blazing in her eyes.

'Jail,' I whispered, as softly as I could.

'Jail?' she shouted. 'Jail!'

By this time the entire café was all ears and looking in my direction. Coffee cups were put down, knives and forks lain to one side. Something interesting was going on.

'For your information,' she began – that was the cue for everyone to cock an ear – 'for your information, I was doing my six weeks for ENSA, you blockhead.'

Peals of laughter filled the room. The sound of conversation and china being clashed against china restarted. I was filled with confusion and tried to look as if I wasn't there. Remembering all the things my mother taught me I moved to apologise to the young lady. When I was a child I had always been told to respect my elders, to take my hat off (if I was wearing one) when people spoke to me and to stand up on a bus if it was full and give my seat to a lady or elderly person. (Something which I still do today. But I don't like accepting a seat from a younger person!)

I plucked up courage and not having a hat on simply bowed gently and said: 'I do apologise for the misunderstanding. I have never heard of ENSA—.'

That was as far as I got.

'Sit down,' she commanded. Her two companions pinched a chair from the next table and I did as she said — I was in the 'pro' circle at last. It seemed she was a singer of some note. Or so she said, to nods of approval from her pro friends. She had been touring in a show and it was the done thing to have six weeks in a year when an artist would be called upon to go and entertain the armed forces. For the last six weeks she had been entertaining the troops with ENSA.

My next question was to change my life.

8

Joining ENSA

'What is ENSA?' I asked.

There were gasps all round. Not only from our table but also from all the others that were within earshot.

'Don't you know?' asked my lady singer.

After it had been established yet again that I hadn't a clue what they were talking about, she explained that many professionals who were not of call-up age worked full time for ENSA, entertaining members of the army, navy, and RAF.

'How old are you?' she asked crisply.

I could feel all eyes were on me.

'Seventeen,' I replied.

'What do you do?'

'I'm a drummer comedian,' I answered. And this time with conviction. I was just going to add that I did impressions when a man at the next table leaned over and said, 'You should get up to Drury Lane, they could do with you, mate.'

'What's in Drury Lane?' I asked in all innocence.

'ENSA!' came the chorus of replies.

I left the Express to a round of applause and shouts of good luck and much laughter. That's what the variety side of show business used to be like – so wonderful for mates. You didn't need to know anyone. If you were in variety you had friends for life. I still have an old mate – today his name is Norman Barratt – the famous ringmaster who is still strutting his stuff all over the world. I met him last year after a thirty-year gap and it was as if we had parted only the day before. Once a variety artist, always a variety artist. It never leaves you and you can't leave it.

I made my way to Drury Lane as fast as my legs could carry me. I found the stage door of the Theatre Royal and the sign above it informed me it was the headquarters of the Entertainments National Service Association – ENSA.

I entered the wide-open doors. To my right was a window looking into a small room where a burly man with a cloth cap was sitting reading a newspaper. I was about to speak to him through the hole in the glass when, without looking up, he said, 'Can I help you, sonny?'

I tried to look as if I was used to doing this sort of thing.

'I'm looking to offer my services as a performer.'

He started to fold up his newspaper neatly and as he did so he gave a rather deep sigh.

'Who do you want to see?' he asked as he heaved himself out of his armchair to come and open the door in front of me.

'Are you an actor or are you Variety?'

My bemused manner didn't go unnoticed by the doorkeeper.

'Variety,' I managed to stutter out.

'What's your act?' his raised voice demanded.

I was sure nothing I could say would convince him of my status as a performer.

'What do you do?' he asked very deliberately and carefully.

The words stuck in my throat.

'On stage!' he bellowed as he advanced towards me. I was ready to cut and run when another voice interceded.

'Can I help?'

The question stopped the doorkeeper in his tracks.

'This chap wants to see someone about performing,' he said in a more respectful tone. 'He's variety, sir.' I noted a slight sneer as he supplied this extra piece of information.

The other voice belonged to a tall, pleasant-faced, grey-haired man with horn-rimmed glasses. He was holding a bundle of papers. As the doorkeeper retreated back to his office kingdom, the man smiled at me.

'Shouldn't you be in the forces?' he asked quietly.

'I'm seventeen, sir,' I replied, a little taken aback.

Smiling once again he added, 'Ah, won't be long. What's your name?'

'Buckland, sir.'

'You can drop the "sir" stuff,' he laughed. 'What do you do?'

Without thinking, and nearly shouting it out, I came back with, 'Drummer comedian.'

'Seventeen?' he mused, half to himself.

He looked long and hard at me and asked if I had a driving licence. I told him firmly that I did.

'Come with me,' he said and, taking my arm, he led me up three flights of stairs to his office. There were many offices, storerooms, and wardrobes all the way up. 'They used to be dressing rooms but we've converted them all for our use,' he explained. 'The glamour days are over at the Theatre Royal for now . . . This is war and the tinsel will have to wait a while.'

He closed the door and asked me to sit down. He took his place behind a trestle table that served as a desk and with a grin he explained who he was.

'My name is Chris Morris and I'm in charge of Light Entertainment. Basil Dean sends his love but he's too busy to greet you so you'll have to put up with me. [I later found out that Basil Dean, actor, producer and film director, was the man responsible for ENSA.] Now, I have an orchestra up in Abergavenny, in Wales, who just happen to need a drummer comedian. It's Charles Kitchen and his orchestra with Muriel Devon – that's his wife – she's the singer. It's a small unit consisting of the band and a comic. The comic who doubles as drummer is being told to pick up his cards as he's too fond of the sauce – and I don't mean tomato.

Charles is a very nice bloke and he won't stand for any nonsense. The problem is nobody drives in the unit except the comic. So you see the problem, no comic, no driver, no show. The driver could be you, and you can be the drummer and the comic – are you up for it?'

Panicking a little, I wondered why he hadn't asked to see my act. But then all he seemed to want was a driver. I decided that the rest would fall into place.

'Are you up for it?' he repeated.

'Yes, oh yes,' I exclaimed trying to conceal my joy.

'You'll get £7 10 shillings a week and we pay your board and lodging – OK? I'll get you a travel warrant. You'll have to be there tomorrow. He got out of his seat to indicate to me that the interview was over. I sat still and he asked me, 'Did you want to say something?'

I gulped, and said, 'I have a small problem.'

He looked up at the ceiling and sighed: 'Go on, tell me the bad news. Your granny's died, or your girlfriend wants to go with you.'

'No, it's nothing like that, Mr Morris. The thing is I haven't been working and I owe some money for my digs,' I gasped in one big rush to get it over as quickly as I could.

'No problem,' he instantly replied. 'Where are you staying? Brixton?'

It was my turn to look at the ceiling.

'No, the Strand Palace Hotel,' I confessed.

This statement was greeted with stony silence and a long stare. Then, he exploded. 'You're not working, you owe money for digs and you're staying WHERE?'

'The Strand Hotel,' I whispered.

Sitting back down in his chair, he shook his head ruefully. 'Even I don't stay at the Strand Palace.' He was almost smiling now. 'How much do you owe?'

Thinking quickly, as I hadn't got my bill yet, I covered myself by saying, 'Seven pounds 10 shillings.'

Giving me a funny look, he reached into his back pocket and produced some folding money. Mr Chris Morris, head of light entertainment, ENSA, opened his mouth to say something, and then changed his mind. Silently, he counted out ten single pound notes instead.

'Send it back to me when you can,' he said, handing me the money with a wink.

To this day I am extremely grateful to that man and thankful for his kindness. He has to accept responsibility for setting me off on the road – not to fame and fortune – but to a life in show business at least. I never met him again. I hope he had a happy life. And, yes, I did send him his £10 back.

I paid my account at the hotel and with money in my pocket I set off the following morning for Wales. I arrived in Abergavenny to be met at the station by Charles Kitchen and his wife. Chris Morris must have phoned to tell them my arrival time. They had a taxi waiting and all three of us drove the short distance to the digs. There I was introduced to the other members of the company.

The man I was replacing was in his fifties, white-haired and, by the look of him, required very little make-up to be a red-nosed comic. Mr Kitchen told me they had a show to do that night at 7.30 p.m. It would be in an army camp somewhere near Abergavenny.

ENSA was set up to entertain the forces wherever they were stationed. It could be at a big army camp or a searchlight with a complement of perhaps only six or seven men and women. It was dark when we set off and the driver, our red-nosed friend, was not the most accomplished navigator. It was not long before we were lost.

In fairness, in those days all you were given was a map but no instructions on how to actually get there because, of course, there were no signposts in the war years. They had all been taken down to confuse the Germans should they ever invade Britain. It was a good idea as it certainly confused us. The headlights on our van didn't help. It was the law that you had to have them covered. Three small slits in each headlight were all you had to see by, and there was no street lighting. If you stopped anyone to ask directions they wouldn't answer you in case you were a member of the fifth column!

Anyway, after an interminable journey through countless Welsh valleys, we found the camp. It was an army supply base and we were doing our show in the NAAFI canteen. It had a nice little stage and as we set up I was able to see who was in my company of artists. There was Charles, Muriel, a guitarist and then the comic – soon to be me – on drums. Not exactly the Count Basie Orchestra.

I was a little underwhelmed at first, but when rehearsals began they made a great sound. I noticed the comic was a fair drummer and Mr Kitchen caught me looking at him and said, as he continued playing, 'You'll be doing that tomorrow night.' I nearly died on the spot. I had been enjoying all the setting up and excitement, but you could have heard a comedy 'gong' when the realisation dawned that in twenty-four hours I would actually have to perform.

The show started on time and there were about two hundred men and women in the audience. The comic announced Charles and the band and he then sat at the drums and played along with them. Muriel came on and sang a couple of numbers – one was Vera Lynn's song 'Always'. This was very popular and it prompted a hearty sing-a-long from the audience.

There was more music by the band and then the comic came out from behind his drums to do his spot. He must have performed for fifteen minutes and his gags went down well. At the end of his act he sang 'We'll Meet Again', another Vera Lynn song. The crowd was shouting for more. I was nervous and excited all at once at the prospect of going on, performing, and getting similar applause.

There were more songs and a second spot for the comic and then a big musical ending to the show. After it was all done we were taken into the officers' mess where a young officer tried to chat up Muriel, only to be told her husband was there too. The officers' mess hospitality was really about us giving them much-needed company. They all tried to turn it into a party but the long-standing ENSA artists had been doing this for too long and as soon as it was possible without causing any offence, they managed to escape.

We made our way back to our digs and a late meal of cold chicken was waiting. We laughed and talked about how the show had gone. Charles suddenly turned to me and said: 'We'll talk in the morning about your spot and what you do, OK?' I told him I would look forward to it and got stuck into the cold chicken.

The following morning I was enjoying a tasty breakfast of bacon and eggs when Charles came in and, pulling up a chair, sat down beside me at the large dining table. We were alone.

'Sleep well?' he asked me.

'Great,' I replied tucking into another slice of bacon.

'Good, well you saw the show last night. What do you think?'

'I thought it was wonderful. The music was great and the comic was quite funny,' I replied.

'No, no, I mean do you think your stuff will fit into the show?' I stopped eating. Suddenly, I didn't feel too hungry any more.

'I'm a bit bothered about fitting in with the musical side of things,' I replied.

'I'm sure you'll be OK. Anyhow, we'll soon find out,' he laughed. 'We have another show tonight. Same place, different audience.'

With that parting shot he grabbed a piece of toast and walked off. So began the longest day of my life.

At five o' clock we all met in the hall. We began loading our props. I was going to wear the dinner suit I had got from a second-hand clothes shop in Oxford months before. It had cost two pounds ten shillings and looked very good to me. I got into our van and placed my outfit carefully on my knees. There was a silence.

'Come on, then,' said a voice. It was Charles Kitchen. He turned in the front passenger seat to look at me sitting behind him. 'It won't drive itself, and none of us can drive.'

Then it hit me. The comic was no longer with us. He had gone to wherever old ENSA comics go. I was now the driver.

'Coming,' was all I could think to say as I climbed into the driver's seat after carefully placing my suit in the back.

I started the engine and, thankfully, had no trouble driving or finding the army camp again. That was the first part of my day completed. We duly set up and waited to begin the show, fortified with cups of tea from a kindly army cook in the kitchens.

The show started with me saying over the microphone: 'Ladies and gentlemen, please welcome "Let's Party" starring Charles Kitchen and his orchestra with Muriel Devon.'

The band started and everyone clapped and cheered as usual. I had been hidden in the wings for the announcement so under cover of a fanfare and all the cheering I slipped into my seat at the drums.

I thought everything was going well and according to plan as I started to play. The opening number was a piece of music written by Charles himself and I had only been playing the drums for a few bars when I saw Charles at the piano looking at me as he played. He was frowning and gently shaking his head from side to side. I smiled back and thought no more of it as I continued to play. The opening number over, he got a few laughs as he fooled about at the piano.

He took his applause and then introduced Muriel. Being keen to show how professional I was I had made a running order: a list of what-follows-what so you know when it's your cue to go on. Muriel singing a song was not on it. I should have known something was wrong because Sammy, the guitar man, slipped onto the piano and started playing Muriel's music. Charles made his exit to the wings where he stood waiting for me to join him. So I did so, only to be grabbed by my lapels and pushed against the bare wall by Charles, who hissed at me in a furious stage whisper. 'You've never played the bloody drums in your life, have you?' He was furious and I was terrified.

'I'm sorry,' I said, standing on tiptoe as he pushed me even harder against the wall his face close up to mine.

'Don't touch the drums again. Just do your two comedy spots,' he said.
'Two?' I bleated.

'Oh God, don't tell me you've only got one!' he cried. I was still on tiptoe and being held by my lapels against the wall.

'It's a full five minutes,' I stated, full of confidence.

As Muriel's singing of 'One Fine Day' was nearing its end I was set down. He rushed back to his piano seat as his wife took her applause and I waited in the wings wondering what I should do next. The band – well, the guitar and part-time piano player – and Charles on the piano again played a few sing-a-long songs with Muriel leading them. The army boys and girls loved it.

Then it came.

'Ladies and gentlemen, I'd like to introduce you to a young man who will shortly be joining you in the armed forces fighting for his country. . .'

Big round of applause here. I joined in and peeped around the curtains to try and see who Charles was talking about . . .

'. . . So please give him a big welcome and make him feel at home . . .'

Charles turned and looked in my direction and it suddenly hit me. He was introducing me.

'. . . Boys and girls, our funny man . . . Glenn Buckland!'

He played a few bars of something or other and I walked out on stage to a gigantic round of applause. Then silence. I started to talk into the microphone. I'd rehearsed my five-minute spot over and over again so I had no fears there but I'd never done it in front of an audience. I was scared I wouldn't get any laughs or, indeed, any reaction. I did get some laughs – well titters really – then I began to go through my impressions: Robb Wilton, the radio comic of the day; Edward G. Robinson, the great tough-guy film star; James Stewart, star of films like *It's A Wonderful Life*, and I finished with Winston Churchill and his speech 'We Will Fight on the Beaches.' I brought the house down. They cheered, they stamped their feet, they clapped.

I walked off stage brimming with confidence. I'd performed my first show. I was a star. Or that's what I thought. I was soon going to be brought down to earth.

The rest of the evening was like a dream. I don't remember what we did or even how we finished it. I do remember the officers' mess afterwards where everyone congratulated me on my impressions. I was on cloud nine.

We travelled back in silence. I parked the van and was the last one into the digs. Our cold supper was laid out and untouched; only Charles Kitchen was in the room, standing, waiting.

'Where is everybody?' I asked.

'Gone to bed. And I'm going too. See you in the morning, Glenn.' Then he quickly left.

There it was again: Glenn Where did that name come from? I was Cecil. Glenn? Actually, I liked Glenn . . . Maybe it was better than Cecil!

I ate a little then went to bed and lay awake dreaming of what might be: Hollywood? The West End? My mind was racing. Then I started to think of what had happened that night. That brought me down to earth. And why had Charles introduced me as Glenn Buckland? I made a mental note to ask him about that in the morning. After what seemed ages I drifted off to sleep, only to be woken by the sound of knocking at my door.

'It's eight thirty and breakfast is getting cold.' I could just about make out the muffled tones of Charles Kitchen.

'Coming,' I shouted, jumping out of bed. A quick wash and no shave later I rushed in. I didn't notice at first that there were only three of us in there. Charles, Muriel and me.

Charles said: 'Grab yourself something before it gets too cold.'

I took a plate and helped myself to one egg and one slice of cold bacon from the sideboard. As I began to eat Charles started talking.

'I should send you back to London, you know.'

I nearly choked on my cold bacon. I stared at him but said nothing.

'We needed a drummer and we got you. We wanted a comic who

could do two spots and you can only do one. You are NOT what we wanted and so, like an unwanted parcel, you should be returned to sender.'

Charles folded his arms and looked me squarely in the face.

'Be honest, this is your first engagement. Am I right?'

I gave a slight nod of the head then explained, 'I needed the job. I had to start somewhere.' To my relief Muriel was smiling.

'We know that, Glenn. That's why we're not going to report you.'

'Oh, thank you, thank you, thank you,' I gushed. I must have sounded like a babbling idiot. But it did the trick.

'We talked it over last night and we think we can mould you into a performer – if you listen to us,' Muriel continued. 'So you can stay, but on one condition.'

'Anything, anything,' I said nervously.

'You never play the drums ever again.' Charles and Muriel said in unison. We all started to laugh.

They told me weeks later that they had gone to their bedroom after my first show and they had argued over my performance – if you could call it that. Muriel was my saving grace. It seems they were never lucky enough to have a family. They had always wanted a boy and as I was a teenager I suppose they must have thought I fitted the bill. No nappies, no bother with primary school or problems at high school to worry about. Here I was, a lost young soul in need of help. For a short period I would be the son they never had. I never had a moment to myself over the next few weeks – they really took me over.

The first task Charles tackled was to tell me my comedy act lacked attack and needed better gags. I also had to find a second spot. I didn't know any more jokes. How would I find another comedy routine? The answer surprised even me.

One morning I came down to breakfast to find Charles sitting with a few sheets of paper in front of him. I thought this was the time to ask the question I had been dying to ask.

'Charles?'

The way I said his name made him look up right away from his papers.

'I've been meaning to ask you. Why did you announce me as Glenn Buckland on that first night and not Cecil?'

'I'd forgotten your first name,' he said, returning his attention to his papers, 'and the only one I could think of was a band leader's. Glenn Miller came to mind so Glenn Buckland came out. Simple as that.'

'Well, I like it.' I said as I poured myself a cup of tea. 'Keep introducing me that way will you?'

As I sat down he pushed the papers in front of him over to me. 'Now you've got that off your chest, Glenn Buckland, read this.'

I looked at the handwritten first few lines. They said: 'Hello, my lovelies. Nice to see you smiling because it's so easy to grin when your ship comes in and life is a happy lot. But the guy worthwhile is the guy who can smile when his shirt creeps up in a knot.'

I looked up at Charles.

'This is our last comic's opening to his act.'

I gasped.

There is an unwritten law in show business – you never use anybody else's material. Not knowingly, that is. I hadn't realised this when Charles had come to me with the answer to our problems. He, of course, knew but didn't tell me! So, with a few changes, I used this material and finished my act with more impressions. After a short spell I found new stories and the act changed a lot. I never touched a drum ever again and after about a month Charles and Muriel said I looked as if I had been doing it for years. I think they were being very kind when they said that.

During my spell with the Charles Kitchen Orchestra I was always looking for a chance to repay their kindness. Charles and Muriel were celebrating their twenty-fifth wedding anniversary and they were going to hold a party on a Saturday night after one of our shows. Everyone was invited: from all of the people at our digs to locals that Charles and Muriel had got to know previous visits. I thought this would be my opportunity.

78

I had a few days to find a present for them and, as ever, money was tight. I pondered what I could possibly get them in my meagre price range when I came across a small jewellers shop in one of the side streets. For a twenty-fifth anniversary I knew the present should be something made of silver. I asked the jeweller if I could see something in silver and he brought out an array of things. They were all way out of my price range. Then something caught my eye in a lovely silk-lined box. It looked so nice, and although it was over my limited budget, I paid my money out in brand-new pound notes and departed with my present tucked under my arm.

I felt like a high-roller. This was the first present I had ever bought for such an occasion. Indeed, I had never been invited to one before. I was so excited I couldn't wait for the party.

That Saturday we came back from another very successful show and everyone was laughing and joking. Charles and Muriel even changed outfits then came down the stairs to a round of applause. Glasses were filled and a toast proposed by Charles's brother, who had got leave from the navy to celebrate with the couple. Then it was time to hand out the wedding-anniversary gifts. Sounds of delight and profuse thanks accompanied the opening of each present. I held back because I wanted mine to be extra special; I owed Charles and Muriel so much.

When I thought everyone else had given presents to the happy couple I stepped forward. Beaming the very best smile that I could manage, I presented my gift to Muriel. She returned my smile and to a chatter of voices she began to open the box. Her expression changed from a wide smile to a wide-eyed stare. This was accompanied by a gasp from the assembled company as she held it up for all to see. The gasps turned to laughter, and the laughter to cheers, and cries of 'Go for it' and 'Good on yer'. This was accompanied by the frenzied shaking of Charles's hand by a few of the men while the ladies giggled and Muriel blushed furiously.

Charles held up his hand and there was silence. 'This has been a wonderful day,' he said. 'Our twenty-fifth wedding anniversary could not have been better. Your gifts are most welcome and you have all gone to so much trouble. Especially our new young company member, Glenn.'

Cheers all round.

'Your gifts are most welcome and we will certainly find a use for them. 'However, the same can't be said for Glenn's beautiful gift of a silver baby's pusher and spoon! If he's trying to tell us something I'm afraid he's too late.'

Laughter and cheers.

I was trying to sneak away when I felt my arm being held. I turned to find Muriel with my gift box in her hand.

'What a lovely thought,' she said, 'you didn't know what it was, did you? We know it's something you simply liked. Well, we love it and we'll always treasure it and its memory. Thank you, Glenn.'

I was mortified. Speechless. I thought it was the biggest faux pas I had ever made in my life. But then, I was only seventeen. Many more would follow . . .

9

A girl called Beryl

It was a short time after the anniversary celebrations that Charles Kitchen told me the bad news: I was to be sent to another unit. Not because I had done anything wrong, but because the Charles Kitchen Orchestra was going to go back to working hotels and were saying farewell to ENSA. This meant I had to join a unit in Devizes in Wiltshire. Once again I was to be the driver and would do two spots in the show. By this time I had made some headway with my act. I was more confident, I was trying different things and I was polishing and smoothing everything. In short, I was learning fast. I set out a more confident and eager artist.

When I arrived in Devizes I found my way to my digs – Blounts Court. It was a large country house that was used as a base for ENSA artists. There I met my new team. First, a small, slightly tubby, man with very thick horned glasses and an outlandish name to match – Teddy Vorsanger. He was probably one of the best piano players and accompanists I have ever known. His wife, who played her violin beautifully and with such tenderness, called herself Violina. What else? They were variety through and through a delightful pair, but always at each other's throats until someone interfered. And then they would join forces against the unfortunate peacekeeper.

It was again a four-handed unit and my introduction to the third member – a dark-haired young lady, very smartly dressed and who had a decidedly posh accent – did nothing to make me feel at home. She smiled and shook my hand politely enough, but even then I had a sense she was not variety as I knew it. She was known as Miss Versatility and, as the name suggests, could sing, act, and, in fact, would do literally anything she was asked to do. She proved this attribute some time later when she agreed to marry me. Her name was Beryl Ratcliffe.

I found out that Beryl had only joined this new unit just before me. She had been in a two-handed unit and had asked for a transfer after being in a couple of bad car accidents through dreadful driving by her unit partner. ENSA was made up like that (not of bad drivers – well, not intentionally!) but of two-handed units consisting of a driver, who had to be a performer, and one other performer, male or female. Then came the four-handed units and the big units – like big bands doing six-week stints. There were all sorts of unit combinations, including plays and actors.

The two-handed unit Beryl was in had played to outlandish places like army searchlight sites. They had the hard job of performing an hour's show between the two of them. They just arrived and performed with no props, no scenery, no stage – nothing. Then they chatted and became hosts after the show.

Over the years a great deal of good-natured fun has been poked at ENSA and its efforts to entertain. But everyone did a sterling job and I have never understood why its work has never been properly recognised along with all the other wartime efforts.

Once again, as the driver, it was my job to ensure we got where we were going safely – still a difficult navigation task in wartime. I can remember stopping to ask the way from a road sweeper in a country lane in the West Country. Beryl was sitting beside me, with Teddy and his wife behind me. I asked Beryl to ask him for directions. She did. He was a very elderly man with a bearded chin which he scratched as he grinned, showing his brown, stained and broken teeth to Beryl.

'Now, that'll be a bit difficult if you're startin' from 'ere.' Beryl was transfixed as he held forth in a beautiful West Country dialect. 'I'll do my best but that'll mean going down yon hill and up t'oth. You'll see yon church by yon graveyard. Go left there and up yon hill. Now after you've gone up yon hill you'll see a sign with nothin' on it pointin' down yon hill. Ah, yon place is hard to find. Best ask at yon church.' With that he turned on his heel and started sweeping his road again.

I managed to thank him as we drove away. I just hope that he didn't hear the roars of laughter as we left. The reason I tell that story is because it became part of our lives. In the coming months, this 'Yon' episode supplied Beryl with her nickname, which sometime later turned into 'Yon Yon'. She was always the one who asked the way in our travels. Years later, when we married, we made a pact. That little episode had such happy memories for us that we said if we ever had a baby girl we would call her Yonnie – and that is exactly what we did. She is now a journalist and features editor.

We'd all joined ENSA to do a job and to entertain those who were fighting for our freedom. When I look back it saddens me to think of the young men and women we entertained and who never made it back to enjoy peace. I'm thinking of one particular show that we did with ENSA in September 1944.

Violina (whose real first name was Pearl, by the way) got a phone call – she was in charge of our unit. She was a very strong-minded lady with a Russian background. Her violin playing of the classics as well as modern pieces would impress today's audiences. She called us all into the lounge of Blounts Court and told us the phone call had been about a show we were being asked to do at short notice. It was to be given the following evening at a secret location. We were to do our usual hour and a half and be ready at six o' clock.

I asked about the venue and was told in typical Violina manner, 'You stupid boy, it's a secret location. We have to be ready and waiting at six tomorrow night.' With that she left without another word.

At 5.45 p.m. the following evening Violina gathered Teddy, Beryl and me in the hall saying: 'Everyone into the van.' We did as she said and sat in silence. I was dying to ask – what happens now? But, I thought better of it after seeing the look on Violina's face. An army motorcycle rider swept into the drive. He rode up to our van and motioned to me to wind my window down. I did so. Above the roar of his motorcycle he shouted: 'ENSA?'

'Yes,' I shouted back.

He waved for me to follow him and we set off at a fair lick along the country roads. He kept slowing down a little to look back to see if I was keeping up with him. My mind was full of speculation about that night's show. Would they be a good audience? How would my act go? Would I get good laughs? Up to now our unit had been in great demand. We had played to different groups of British army and US forces as well. The Americans were great laughers. In fact, looking back, I got some of my best laughs from the American soldiers. When they laughed, they really laughed and laughed some more. Today's comics seem to have a problem with the so-called difference in British and American humour. I don't think there is a difference. If something is funny, it will get a laugh. If it's not, it won't. The problem with some young comedians today is many of them are simply not funny. They say funny things but *they* are not funny. They depend too much on the gag. People laugh today at the image of Sir Harry Lauder but way back then he played in the US to great success. Who says British humour doesn't travel? Danny Kaye? Ricky Gervais? Do me a favour.

After some time my motorcycle escort turned into what looked unsurprisingly like an army camp. We pulled up at a Nissen hut and a young officer greeted us. It wasn't until much later we found out we were going to entertain the 1st Airborne Division who, of course, we now know suffered terrible casualties in 1944. The young officer took us inside and said we were to use this as our base until we did the show. He introduced himself as the entertainment officer Lieutenant Michael Richards. He told us to help ourselves to the tea and sandwiches they had laid on in case we hadn't eaten. He then apologised for having to leave us and said he would return to take us to the stage area when everything was ready.

When he left, Teddy Vorsanger, who had been in show business since goodness knows when, said: 'His name was Richards. I wonder if he's any relation to Cyril Richards, the West End musical and revue star?' We never thought any more about it, made ourselves some tea, and sat around nervously waiting for the call. It came in the shape of Lieutenant Richards.

'I'd better explain what the situation is,' he began. 'We are part of Operation Market Garden, an airborne force that was due to go into action tonight. Unfortunately, the weather has deteriorated and, as we are going into Holland by glider and with paratroopers, the weather is all-important. We have been delayed and so we'll be going in during daylight early tomorrow morning. The boys are a bit uptight; we thought you could come along and make the time go a bit quicker for them.'

We told him that that's what we'd do and we set off after him as he led us to what looked like a very large hangar. We were not prepared for what we saw. It was the noise that hit you first. If you have ever seen an American boxing match on television that's what the noise was like. The sight that greeted us inside made us all gape. There was a mobile stage in the centre and there were hundreds and hundreds of soldiers packed around it. At one end of the hall were countless barrels of beer. Men were helping themselves to foaming mugs and glasses of it. Some were standing, some sitting cross-legged, most had a glass or mug of beer. Lieutenant Richards made a path for us through the Red Devils, and as soon as they saw our two female members, the whistles and cheers increased in volume. We walked single file behind the lieutenant as he led us to a small room to one side of the hall. This was to be our dressing room, or waiting area. It would mean we would have to fight our way back through this multitude of laughing, singing, chattering men to reach the stage to perform. Nothing was ever easy on ENSA duty.

As we braced ourselves for what was to come Lieutenant Richards coughed gently.

'I think we should start. Are you ready?'

We said nothing, I think we must have looked a little scared because he said, 'Don't worry, I'll introduce you. Good luck.'

His appearance was greeted with a mixture of boos and cheers. Announcing they would now be entertained by an ENSA group was the signal for the boos and cheers to increase in volume along with laughter – it was obviously all good-natured banter. There were more cheers as the lieutenant left the stage to sit and enjoy what we had to offer.

Teddy Vorsanger started the show with a selection of well-known melodies. He could make a piano sound like a full orchestra in the pit of a theatre. Teddy took a deep breath. 'Wish me luck,' he said as he stepped out into the unknown.

The noise was unbelievable. After climbing over bodies and legs he reached his piano and started to get things going with 'Ain't We Got Fun.' The words of the chorus are: 'Every morning, every evening, ain't we got fun.' We all looked at each other in the waiting room. You could say that again!

After a few bars the noise began to die down. They began to sing along, even if they didn't know the words, to songs like 'When Day is Done.' Those that already knew the words were at full voice: 'Although I miss your tender kiss, the whole day through, I miss you most of all when day is done.'

Violina gave Beryl and me a little pep talk while Teddy was getting the show started.

'Go out and do your best. These boys need us to take their minds off what they are being asked to do.' She emphasised this with a shake of her fist at us. We needed no prompting.

Teddy finished his opening spot with 'Roll Out the Barrel' – a sure-fire winner. He came off to tremendous cheers and applause. We were off to a good start and by this time many had stopped drinking and some were even making a space for an aisle so that we could make our way back and forth to the stage.

Violina was next on the bill. She flounced out onto the stage without a flicker of fear on her face. She looked at them, held her violin out at arms length – commanding silence – and got it! She turned to Teddy at the piano, smiled and he started to play the intro to one of her very fine, fast, and furious, gypsy-style solos. She continued to the stamping of a thousand feet along with cheers and whistles – not to mention applause. It was wonderful to hear. The atmosphere was electric. It is not often you see grown men cry, but we saw many of them doing so that night.

Beryl was next. Up to now it had been music and audience participation. This was new territory. She had specially written songs with patter included. We call this a 'point number'. The question was would they listen? It's very hard to quieten an audience down when they are on a high so she had a tough job on her hands. Violina took her applause and introduced, 'Our young Beryl Ratcliffe.'

Whistles and cheers greeted her walk on stage in a beautiful, full and flowing, off-the-shoulder evening gown. She sang her opening number, which went down well judging by the whistles and applause. Then she went into one of her comedy numbers where she sang and talked in different dialects. To do this type of performance you need a certain amount of attention or the humour is lost. As there were men from all over the UK it was listened to with interest and they laughed in the right places. Then, after taking her applause, she went into her finishing number. She wore a blue dress and so her final song was 'Alice Blue Gown', the hit number from the great Broadway show *Irene*. The sheet music has an instruction just above the music line that says 'slowly and tenderly' and that's just the way she sang it – to obvious effect. As she was ending her song, soldiers were trying to touch the hem of her dress; many of them were in tears.

The reaction was amazing. She had great difficulty in getting off the stage to make way for me. I attempted to meet her halfway. We crossed, she making for our little room, me for the stage. I had no song to start with, just right in with my first gag. By this time I was learning to handle an audience and so I took this as a challenge. I had an act to do and they were going to listen. They did. My gags went down well. I even began to ad lib and I had them on my side. I got to my impersonation of Winston Churchill and I wondered if it would be the wrong thing to include on such an occasion. How wrong could I be? They wouldn't stop cheering, stamping their feet, whistling and clapping.

The whole show was a riot. Not because we did anything different – it was purely because of the situation. These men were going to war the next morning, not knowing what they were about to face. If ever I need a definition of the word courage I will always remember that night. We did an hour and a half on stage and after the show, in our small room, Lieutenant Richards thanked us and told us they had word that the weather was clearing and they would be able to leave by gliders first thing. As he prepared to leave he said, 'I'm very sorry, but you can't leave until we've gone in the morning. We've arranged accommodation for you.'

This took the wind out of our sails; we asked why.

'I'm afraid it's a case of national security. You can't make any phone calls or contact anyone in any way. Sorry.'

We accepted the situation and followed our very polite and helpful lieutenant to a large house they were using as headquarters. We were given three rooms and told breakfast would be laid on for us. We thanked Lieutenant Richards who had been looking after us so well. He smiled and said, 'Thank you for the show and good luck.'

We never saw him again and, much later, found out he had been killed in action during this mission – part of the massive Battle of Arnhem. You can imagine how upset we all were at this news.

The following day we left in our van. The place was now like a ghost town with just the odd guard to wave us through the main gate. We found our way back to Blounts Court and continued with our normal shows feeling more than a little deflated. After all the excitement of the Red Devils experience we had to come down to earth, I suppose. The war had suddenly come home to me. And it wouldn't be long before I'd be reporting for national service.

I had many happy days with this ENSA unit and some hairy ones as well. I remember going to do a show in the Dungeness area of the country. It's between Folkestone and Hastings on the south coast and is now a nature reserve. But way back in 1944 this was an army-controlled area. I was driving the car and, as usual, there were no signs to tell us where we were or, indeed, where we were going to or from. I was lost.

I had tried a few roads without seeing any signs of Nissen huts when I spotted a huge area of open land ahead that led down to the English Channel. I saw what looked like a hut that was camouflaged army-style to deceive enemy planes. I decided to make for it and ask the way.

With cries from my fellow artists in the van of, 'Are you sure of where you're going?' and 'Are we lost?', I put my foot down on the accelerator and hoped for the best. I made my way down a very narrow lane that led me into open ground and I could see the hut was still a long way in the distance as we bumped and rolled over the rough, grassy terrain. I began to wonder why anyone would put a hut miles out in the middle of nowhere like this.

We eventually got to the hut and I climbed out of the van to find it was a very ramshackle affair. It had no doors and more importantly, no sign of life. I turned to walk back to the van when there was the most almighty explosion that knocked me flat on my face. Through shocked eyes I saw a deep smoking hole a few feet away. I ran back to the van. Amid screams and another 'What a bloody war,' from Teddy, I slammed the van into gear and headed back the way I thought I'd come.

I could see something that looked very like the hut I had just left in front of me so I made for that. Going fairly fast I pulled up beside – not a hut – but a Sherman tank. I got out and walked towards it, laying one hand on the tank to steady myself. I was still a bit shaken up. That was nothing to how I felt when the tank fired its gun in the direction I had just come from in my van. The vibration from the tank threw me to the ground and as I was trying to get up a head popped out from the tank's turret.

'Are you trying to get yourself killed?' the tank driver shouted.

I tried to look as unconcerned as I could and managed to stutter out, 'I was looking for an army base.'

The tank driver took his helmet off revealing a very ruddy face with bright blue eyes.

'Well, you certainly found one,' he replied.

'Where are we?' I asked him.

'On the practise firing range for our tanks,' said a man who was now standing beside me.

I had been so shaken up the situation that I failed to notice the young officer who had joined me by the tank.

'You were damned lucky you weren't all killed,' he said, nodding in the direction of our van. 'Didn't you see the red flag? You were standing right by our target. It's a good job Johnny spotted you.'

I won't repeat what my fellow ENSA artists said to me later back in the van.

This was just one of the hazards of entertaining the troops during wartime. On one occasion we were performing in a Nissen hut not far from Dover when one of the audience jumped up yelling 'Doodle Bug! Doodle Bug!'

The music stopped and there was utter silence. Over two hundred people were as still as stone. All you could hear was a 'putt, putt, putt' sound like an old motorbike. It got louder and louder. We all remained stock-still. Then it faded away and everyone started to clap with relief but we also knew it was on its way to London where it would stop 'putt, putting' all of a sudden and cause death and destruction for some poor souls as it dived to earth.

As Teddy Vorsanger said, what a bloody war.

The gatherings in the officers' mess after a show were part of the job of an ENSA artist. It gave the officers a chance to forget the war for a while and chat about everyday things. They would serve tea and goodies for us and they'd break the ice by asking us questions about the show. I was often asked if I knew a chap who had entertained at their camp by the name of Peter Sellers. My honest answer was always a simple 'no'. It would seem he did an act rather like mine. While I did gags and impressions of well-known stars and people of the day like Winston Churchill and the great Robb Wilton, he would impersonate people of his own invention. It was amazing how many camps brought up his name. The usual remark to start the conversation was, 'You're very like that chap Peter Sellers.' To be quite honest I got a bit fed up with it, as I was able to tell Peter some time later when I met him for the first time. What's incredible is that he told me the same story. The camps he played asked *him* if he'd heard of a chap called Glenn Buckland. It was a small world.

The ENSA unit I shared with Teddy, Violina and Beryl was a happy one and we loved all the hours of travelling and entertaining the troops. The war looked to be going our way and everyone lived in the hope that it wouldn't be long before peace. My war, on the other hand, was about to start.

10

The reluctant airman

It was about this time that I heard my mother and father were reunited and were once again employed as a butler and cook – this time for a 'lady in waiting' to the old Queen Mary, Lady Cynthia Colville at Cheyne Walk in Chelsea. Mum sent on a letter that had arrived for me at their Chelsea address telling me to report to Fulham Labour Exchange to register for my national service. It looked like my days in ENSA were coming to an end.

I arrived on the appointed day at Fulham Labour Exchange to be greeted by a very nice man with glasses perched on the end of his nose and wispy grey hair. After a pleasant 'good morning', he turned over a few papers, took one out of the pile and settled himself on his stool behind his high counter.

'Now,' he said in a voice that, despite it's soft tone, still resonated with doom to me, 'you are Cecil Edward Buckland, are you not?'

My first thought was to deny it. My second was, what happened to Glenn?

'You have to register for your national service I'm afraid,' he said, shaking his head. 'Do you have a preference for a particular service?'

'No,' I said. Then I asked, 'Do I have a choice?'

'Yes, of course you do,' He smiled warmly. 'You can choose between the army, navy or air force or (shaking his head again) you could go down the mines.'

Peering at me over the top of his glasses, he awaited my reply.

The last choice had taken me by surprise. I had visions of being able to work in a show in the evenings and go to work in the mines during the day.

'I'll take the mines,' I said.

He nearly fell off his stool. He leaned towards me: 'I shouldn't really be saying this, but have you really considered this?'

I had to confess that up to a few moments before, I hadn't. He then painted a dire picture for me of what it would be like down a coal mine. I could almost feel the cold and damp as he described the grim scene far below the ground.

'The Royal Air Force is a fine service,' I heard him say.

'Right.' My head was suddenly full of visions of the dashing pilots of the day. 'It's the Brylcream boys for me,'

'You will not be disappointed,' my mentor said, smiling as if he had just sold me a car. Passing a slip of paper to me his final comment was: 'Good luck, son.'

If he were alive today I would shake him by the hand and thank him for saving my life. Looking back I suspect he tried to give advice to many a young lad who came his way. I will always remember him.

I returned to the ENSA unit and did many more shows and was very happy until one day a letter arrived telling me to report to RAF Padgate, near Warrington, on 14 August 1945. It was the day the war with Japan ended. How lucky can you be?

I said my goodbyes to Teddy, Violina and Beryl and, with sadness, made my way back to London. I stayed at the YMCA and met Mum and Dad on their day off. My father couldn't wait to tell me how he'd locked Queen Mary in his butler's pantry at Cheyne Walk while she was visiting Lady Cynthia Colville. It seems Her Majesty had asked him if she could see his new pantry. She, apparently, made a habit of concerning herself with such matters. Dad, being afraid of nothing or no one, requested she looked for herself. As Queen Mary entered the small pantry (only Dad could do it) he pulled the door shut and locked it. It would seem this amused the Queen no end and, amidst much laughter, when he unlocked the door the Queen remarked – in somewhat Dick Emery style – 'Buckland, you are awful!'

I decided to get a haircut before I reported for service at Padgate because so many people had been telling me that if you arrived with long hair they just chopped it off. I thought I would pre-empt the hair harvest so I went to a hairdressers in Charing Cross Road. I think it was called Strangs.

'You have to take more off. I need it to be very short,' I kept telling the man who was cutting my hair. I've always been inclined to wear my hair fairly long so it was a struggle to tell him to cut more off. But he did as I asked each time – more, then a little more, then even just a little bit more after that. By this time my barber was nearly in tears.

'No more, please, no more,' he pleaded.

I looked in the mirror and saw myself with a very, very close-cropped head. My barber gave me the slip for payment at the desk and changed from his white coat into the jacket of a very expensive-looking Saville Row suit. I held out a ten-shilling note as a tip for him. He took it with the air of someone who expected more. I followed him down the stairs and paused to pay my bill. The young girl looked at my slip and said: 'Seven pounds ten shillings please.' I nearly died. It was more than my bill at the Strand Palace all those months ago. As I left with wobbly legs I noticed my barber friend slipping behind the wheel of a brand new sports car and zooming off. I wondered briefly if I should reconsider a career in show business and train to be a hairdresser . . .

The trip to Padgate was uneventful but I did notice many young men of my age on the train. I arrived at the gates of RAF Padgate in convoy with many others – most from the same London connection. We all stood in line to present our tickets and prove our identity. A warrant officer was waiting for us on the other side of the gate.

'Fall in,' he growled.

About twenty of us looked at one another in bewilderment.

'Get in line . . . ONE . . . AFTER . . . THE . . . OTHER.'

We all shuffled into some sort of line and moved off after him. We were taken to a building where we were kitted out and told to get dressed and be outside in ten minutes flat. After what seemed like an hour we all gathered outside and stood in a rough line. A uniformed man was standing watching us with his hands behind his back

'You don't know me,' he said, 'but I know who you all are and it's going to be my job to turn you from the rabble you are now into airmen. I am Flight Sergeant McBride and my first job is to see you represent the Royal Air Force as a smart body of men.'

I had a feeling we were going to hear a lot from this man.

'First. Hats off . . . NOW!'

Instantly, we all did as we were told. He turned on his heel and marched to the end of our line. 'Look to the front,' he barked.

He walked behind us, tapping each man on the shoulder with the words 'OK' or 'haircut'. I received a 'haircut' – I couldn't believe my ears! Haircut? ME? I had just spent seven pounds ten shillings on getting my hair cropped to my scalp and he wanted me to get a haircut . . . He emphasised this by pushing his face right into mine and bellowing, 'First thing in the morning, camp barber!'

We were marched to our hut and bunk beds. I sat on the lower bunk of a double and thought, 'I am an airman.' I was 2231183 A/C Second Class Cecil Buckland.

The next six weeks were a nightmare for me. I was taught to march, to peel potatoes, to salute, and to say 'sergeant' or 'sir' to anything that moved. The one thing that gave me the fright of my life was grenade practice. We had one man in our batch who was a terrible timekeeper. He was always late, his marching was out of step and he was always just that fraction behind everyone else.

Now at grenade practice this was a problem that could affect all of us. The training sergeant instructed us, 'You have to hold your grenade in your right hand, take the pin out with your left, and bring your arm over your head in an arc and throw it as far as you can away from you.'

Fine in principle. The only thing was that our unfortunate comrade had a habit of bringing his arm over his head but always hitting his head with his arm. The result was he'd drop the grenade and the grenade would roll back down into the pit where the instructor and all of us were waiting for our turn to throw. The danger was minimal when using dummy grenades, so when the time came for him to use a live one we all said our prayers. He did what he always did – fluffed it. The grenade rolled back down into our pit. Like lightning our instructor grabbed the grenade, flinging it as far as he could. We all ducked down amidst a shower of earth and stones from the explosion that followed. Our likeable lad looked at the instructor and said, with tears in his eyes, 'I can't stand it.'

'No,' said the instructor, 'Neither can we, lad – you're excused practice.' We all breathed a sigh of relief.

It was a lonely time for me. I wasn't a 'mix in quick' type of lad like most of the other new recruits. Any spare time I had, I spent in nearby Warrington. The theatre there used to put on touring shows like *Happidrome*. This was adapted for the stage from the original broadcast production courtesy of the BBC and starred Harry Korris as Mr Lovejoy and Robbie Vincent as Enoch. They were famous names on the radio at that time and had headlined a variety bill.

One act I recall doing a spot in *Happidrome* was Mackenzie Reid and Dorothy – billed as 'Scotland's Ace Accordionists'. The theatre would have a variety bill or revue every week and I can remember seeing a Sunday concert starring the 'new singing sensation and actress', Petula Clark. She would have been about ten years old then and was dressed in a long taffeta dress that was too big for her. The audience of mostly airmen from the camp loved her.

I was sitting in the pub beside the theatre one night having my usual half pint when the door burst open to cries of 'drinks all round'. It was the revue company from the theatre who had rushed in after their show to get a quick drink before the pub closed. The one who had cried for the drinks was dressed in a camel-hair coat with a belt tied in a knot – the same way I always wore my coats. I had seen gangsters in films wear their coats like that and I thought it was the 'in' thing to do (I still do it today, over sixty years on).

The camel-coat gent was full of vim and vigour, laughing and joking with all around him. The show they were all in was called *Soldiers in Skirts* an all-male revue starring Charles Regan and Max Carolle. The gent in the camel-haired coat was Max Carolle, born Daniel Patrick Carroll and better known today as Danny La Rue.

My days at Padgate came to an end when I got my first posting. The travel warrant said I was going to Bircham Newton in Norfolk – not far from Sandringham, with King's Lynn being the nearest town. I arrived at the small RAF camp wondering what I would be doing for the war effort given that the conflict had ended on 14 August the previous year. I felt it was all going to be a bit of an anti-climax both for me and for king and country. But I decided I would do my best as a national-service airman. There were three of us posted there from Padgate, so at least I knew people. We settled in quite well and were made welcome by the airmen and women at the camp. There were always notices up in the NAAFI canteens telling us about numerous activities we could do in our spare time.

During a cup of tea one afternoon I spotted a notice that asked for volunteers for a show the camp was putting on. It was being devised and produced by a Sam Hubbard. I found Sam rehearsing in the theatre he'd made up from scrounging bits and pieces, creating a stage and all you required in a disused Nissen hut. He had a professional air about him and I discovered that he had put on shows for some time at the camp. This latest one was to be called *You've Had It* (a well known RAF expression). He even had programmes printed in blue just like real theatre ones:

RAF Station Bircham Newton presents its latest revue, 'You've Had It,' devised and produced by Sam Hubbard (by kind permission of Commanding Officer Group Captain J. Norwood).

After a chat with Sam it was agreed I would be welcome as a member of this new revue.

My duties at Bircham Newton were not defined. As an A/C 2 I had no qualifications. So, after a few days of wandering around, sweeping up and spud bashing in the cookhouse, I was called into the CO's office. Group Captain Norwood told me that he had heard from Sergeant Sam Hubbard about how I was going to perform with 'the boys'. I said I was delighted and then he hit me with the big one.

'Seeing as you're going to be doing the show,' he said, 'you'll need some time off your work. What are you doing at the moment?'

'General Duties, sir,' I said.

'Report to the medical section in the morning. They'll show you the ropes.'

He drew attention to the fact that the interview had now ended by slamming the book in front of him shut. I saluted and marched out of the office. Now we had a problem. I couldn't stand the sight of blood. Being told I was to work in the medical section was like being told I was going to face bullets. Actually, forget the bullets – the blood was worse!

I never slept that night so I looked a little rough when I reported to the medical section the following morning. The white-coated sergeant who greeted me was pleasant enough. He pointed to a short, white coat hanging on the door.

'Put that on and follow me,' he instructed. He led me down a corridor to a room where a group of people were washing their hands. 'Scrub up,' he commanded. I must have looked blank because the next order was 'Wash your hands.' I moved to a washbasin and did as I was told. 'Ready?' the sergeant enquired.

I nodded only because I couldn't speak.

He opened a door, stood back and waited for me to go ahead. I walked in to be met by a group of white-coated people and a naked man on the table in front of them. One of the coats stepped towards me with a bucket in his hand. 'Empty this, will you?' he said. I peered in the bucket, which was half full of blood.

I blacked out. When I came round the white coats had gone and just one – the sergeant – was leaning over me. 'You gave us a bit of a fright,' he said.

'It's the blood . . . I can't stand the blood,' I mumbled.

He laughed and said: 'It wasn't blood, just red water. It was a joke. We always do that to new recruits but didn't think you'd pass out on us.'

I did work in the medical section but only in the office and I think that was possibly more for their benefit than mine. I wasn't very happy in my job and the only time I came to life was when I was rehearsing for our new show. I had been thinking about the people I had met on ENSA for some time and I decided to write to them. I picked on Beryl by chance as she was the only one whose address I had taken. I wrote telling her about our show and what I was doing at the camp and asked what she was up to.

Much to my surprise she wrote back telling me she was working with a famous double act of the day – Dave and Joe O'Gorman. They were among the founders of the Variety Artists Federation (VAF) later to amalgamate with Equity, the actors' trade union. She told me they were playing in variety theatres all over the country. In response, I invited her down to see the opening night of our revue. Again, to my surprise, she accepted.

I was doing a single spot in the show. My bill matter in the programme said I was a 'Dickens' of a comedian. I'd got together material that was quite funny and I was working my character voices into the act, including some characters from Charles Dickens. It was going well. I also worked in the sketches and did a couple of songs and musical numbers. It was a good enough show to play theatres. The group captain invited local people to the performances and many stayed for a late dance with music by our very own Blue Gremlins Swingette, with a charming young WAAF vocalist.

Beryl had arranged to stay at the local pub and it was a terrific evening

Things moved quite fast with Beryl and me after that. A couple more visits from her and I decided to take the plunge. I had noticed she always wore a very nice diamond ring her father had given her. I asked if she fancied getting engaged. I told her I could not afford a ring but if she would agree to put her father's ring on her right finger, one day I might be able to afford a proper one.

The cheek worked. The ring changed fingers. She carried on working and I carried on RAF-ing. Then I was notified that I had a posting to RAF Halton, the top medical centre for the RAF. I was classed as a medical orderly on the books, even though I never saw a ward. The pen-pushers didn't know that. We were right in the middle of doing another revue at Bircham Newton when the bombshell came. Everyone tried to get me off being posted – even the group captain. But it was no use. I was off.

I arrived to find Halton vastly different from Bircham. Everything was geared towards providing first-class hospital attention. I was marched in to see my new commanding officer who had been a top-class surgeon in Civvy street and who turned out to be a very, very nice man. The upshot of my interview was that, unlike at Bircham Newton, I found out that the chain of command went up a long way. This was a squadron leader. After a pep talk – which I knew he must have given a thousand times – I was dismissed. I reported to the main medical room in the building and was soon found work to do. It was a case of General Duties again – only this time I was doing all the mucky jobs that could be passed on from others in the hospital. I was given nothing medical to do at all.

By this time Mum and Dad had changed jobs yet again. They were now in Harley Street. In fact, sheer chance found them working for the top medical man in the RAF. His title was head of medical services.

This news sparked the germ of an idea in my head. Sam Hubbard at Bircham Newton had been telling me to apply for a transfer to Squadron Leader Ralph Reader's RAF Gang Shows in London and he would vouch for my being talented enough to be a Gang Show member. I obtained some leave and visited Mum and Dad in their new position, which came with a very nice flat attached to it. We talked about a lot of things then we came to my being in the RAF, and what I was doing, and I told them of my horror of anything medical. The upshot of this conversation was that Dad disappeared upstairs to talk to his boss. In a short time he came back down and said I was to go up as his boss wanted to see me.

It was almost like talking to my own doctor. He asked me all sorts of questions but mainly about what sort of work I was doing at Halton. I told him I was doing no good in the medical section of the RAF and I would be of more use to the service if I could get a transfer to RAF Gang Shows, where I could use any talent I had to much greater effect. He listened and his final words to me were: 'Go back to your unit and continue your work.'

I returned to Halton and continued my General Duties. About a week after my trip to London I was in the office filing some papers when a sergeant came in. He looked at the two WAAF girls at their desks, then at me and asked, 'You A/C 2 Buckland?'

'Yes, sergeant, 2231183,' I responded.

He gave me what could only be described as a very funny look. 'The CO wants to see you.'

The girls looked up from their desks expectantly. The sergeant spotted them. 'Get on with your work,' he said curtly.

'Best follow me,' he said, glaring at me again.

I tried to keep up with him as he speed–walked ahead of me. We ended up in a part of the camp that I'd never been to before. After climbing two flights of stairs the sergeant turned sharply and snapped at me.

'Wait here.'

He entered the doorway ahead of us. I was left standing on one leg then the other, feeling the strain after our hundred-yards dash. The sergeant returned and barked out, '2231183 A/C Buckland, SIR.'

He gave a sharp nod of his head for me to enter the open door of the room he'd just left. I was confronted by the CO – and not the squadron leader I had seen on my arrival. This was the big cheese. I recognised a group captain when I saw one, and I stood to attention as best as I could.

The mature figure in uniform looked up at me from behind his huge desk. 'Stand easy, Buckland,' he commanded. I attempted to carry out his instruction. 'So [a very long pause] you don't like it here? [Another very long pause]. Cat got your tongue?'

No, I thought. I'm just shitting myself. Was I about to be court-martialled?

The group captain sat back in his leather armchair and studied me closely. 'Why don't you like it here? Speak freely,' he added.

'It's not that I don't like it, sir, it's more that the job doesn't like me. I faint at the first sign of blood, sir.'

'Hmm,' he said.

And again, this time longer in duration, 'Hmmmmmm.'

He leaned forward and looked at the paper in front of him. Then he leaned back in his chair. After a while, he leaned forward again.

'Hmm,'

Here it comes again I thought.

'Hmmm.'

I was right.

He looked up at me.

'Well, I think we have a problem. If we were on a wartime footing I wouldn't be talking to you. You would be in the field helping anyone who wanted medical attention without you worrying about seeing blood. In fact, we could very soon cure you of your blood problem. But, we have more important things to do here than worry about you. I understand you're a stage performer and you think you would be better employed entertaining our RAF men and women than trying to save their lives on an operating table where the blood would, upset you, no doubt.'

He raised his eyebrows at me and leaned back in his chair yet again. 'I have a recommendation here asking me to release you from Halton

Medical Centre and transfer you, subject to their agreement of course, to the RAF Gang Show in London.

'As you are only A/C 2 General Duties,' he leaned forward and picked up a pen, 'I will agree to your transfer. Expect to leave in due course. Dismissed.'

He looked up and his face broke into a smile: 'Good luck.'

'Yes, sir, thank you, sir,' I turned on my heels and walked as calmly as I could out of his office.

The waiting sergeant said: 'Back to your work, son.' Then he turned and walked away.

I was alone out in the open air. I made my way back to the office where I had been filing papers such a short while ago. Although I admire and respect all the wonderful work the medical boys and girls did in the RAF, I would have only been a hindrance. The stage was calling me back once again.

11

Back in showbiz with the Gang Show

The RAF Gang Shows HQ was in Knightsbridge in London. I found it just around the corner from Harrods. You walked up a couple of flights of stairs and into a small, flat-type dwelling and there you were. When I knocked on the door a voice invited me to enter. There seemed to be a small number of people working at desks and at filing cabinets. An airman in uniform at the main desk looked up and said: 'Can I help you?'

I produced my papers from Halton and gave them to him.

'Ah ... A/C 2 Buckland. Yes, we know all about you. Welcome to Gang Shows.'

Before I could answer a voice boomed from a room on my left-hand side that had an open door.

'Come in, come in!'

'On you go,' said the airman, smiling.

I walked into the room to see a pilot officer seated at his desk. I sprang to attention and saluted.

'2231183 A/C 2 Buckland, sir.'

'Oh bugger that. You can forget all that officer rank stuff here,' he said as he put out his hand for me to shake. I shook it with a huge smile on my face.

'I'm Frank Thornton,' he said. 'We have all the gen about you and we're a bit thin on the ground so you'll be joining a Gang as soon as possible. Come along with me and I'll introduce you.'

He led me back into the larger area where many people were working and introduced me to them. As I was shaking hands with one of my new colleagues, another airman came into the room.

'Ah, here's one of our artists who's working in the office at the moment,' said the airman who was still holding my hand in a vice-like grip. I disentangled myself from this enthusiastic welcome with some difficulty. I later discovered he was one of the best female impersonators in the business. He became a good pal of mine during my Gang Show days.

I turned my attention to the slightly tubby, rather round-faced bushy-headed young man who had just entered. We shook hands. 'I'm Sellers,' he said, 'Peter Sellers. Welcome to Gang Shows.' Peter later told me he'd shrewdly got himself into the office in London to enable him to make contacts in the business for when he was demobbed. Being stationed in London he could keep tabs on what was going on in show business. At my first visit to Cadogan Gardens I had expected to meet the great Ralph Reader but, no, that would come later. I was taken into a part of the building that was used as a wardrobe. It was well stocked with all sorts of costumes and I was shown the outfit I was expected to wear as a Gang Show member. Grey trousers, grey striped shirt, and a red scarf that had to be worn around the neck in a cravat style. I was told my own 'uniform' would be waiting for me when I got to my new posting at Chessington – a surprise to me, as I had no idea that there was an RAF station so close to London.

The other members of my Gang Show unit met me when I arrived. Tim Dormond was in charge and he was a big guy who looked rather like Burt Lancaster. Tim came from a famous circus acrobatics family. His father and uncle used to have a comedy tumbling act that toured the music halls. Another member was Jock Kerr, a tough little Scot who had the voice of Mario Lanza. If you can picture Mickey Rooney when he was in *Babes in Arms*, that was Jock. Unlike Mickey Rooney he couldn't dance for toffee, but boy, could he sing. He'd never been trained to sing but Jock always said he had a 'pub' voice and that up in his beloved Glasgow there were a great many just like him. In later years I was to find out the truth of this claim for myself. Willie Watson, our piano player was, always dying to play the classics but having to make do with songs like 'Crest of a Wave', the signature tune of the Gang Shows. The tune was written by Ralph Reader, a talented producer and director who had refused offers to do musicals in Hollywood so that he could do his own thing and also help the war effort. I still remember the words:

> We're riding along on the crest of a wave and the sun is in the sky
> All our eyes on the distant horizon, look out for passers-by
> We'll do the hailing while other ships can do the sailing
> We're riding along on the crest of a wave and the world is ours.

The first thing I had to do was learn the words and movements for this opening chorus. I was given a sheet of paper set out as follows:

Instructions for opening chorus:
We're riding along [performing a bouncing movement of the body]
On the crest of a wave [as if riding a horse]
And the sun is in the sky [pointing skywards]
All our eyes on the distant horizon [hands over eyes as if looking into the distance]
Look out for passers-by
We'll do the hailing, while other ships can do the sailing [wave hand to front, then wave hand in a wavy motion]
We're riding along on the crest of a wave and the world is ours.

This was all very helpful to those who had never put one foot in front of the other on a stage. The Gang Shows comprised those who could sing, play instruments, yodel, or perhaps do magic tricks. But many had never had to do production scenes like an opening chorus. 'Keep it simple' was Ralph Reader's motto, and it worked.

The impact was incredible, however, whenever a professional performer found their way into the shows. These included the likes of Dick Emery, Peter Sellers and Frank Thornton. It was remarkable how quickly their influence would lead to a unit taking on the air of a professional company; you can begin to understand how valuable they were to Gang Shows. You had a mixture of people who loved the theatre and it was a great way for anyone with talent to be demobbed and try their luck treading the boards.

An amazing number of comics came out of the armed forces looking for work in show business after the Second World War. Today it's singers and groups who try for fame and fortune. My advice to aspiring performers is: if you have talent, the money will find you. Keep persevering and learning your craft.

Chessington was a real eye-opener for me because I was mixing with a very modern professional in Tim Dormond. He knew the theatre well from his circus background and had friends like Bonar Colleano. Bonar was very much in demand in films and had the looks of a matinee idol. He used to come down to see Tim a lot while we were rehearsing at Chessington and we got to be a trio. Bonar would turn up on a sunny Saturday around midday and con his way past the guard at the gate to pick us both up in his open-top American sports car. It was huge with a large boot.

One day I said to him: 'What do you keep in the boot . . . another car?'

Tim and I roared with laughter when he replied: 'No, my motorbike.' He opened up the boot to show us his mini-bike, took it out and unfolded it. Bonar had somehow got hold of one of the mini-bikes that paratroopers had used after parachuting down into enemy territory. He used it to get around the West End on a busy day; he would park the car, get the bike out of the boot, and set off ducking and diving through the stationary traffic.

Everyone looked at him as he sped by with his long legs sticking out. He loved the attention – and the mini-bike. Sad to say he never let Tim or me have a go. Unfortunately, he died, far too young, in a car crash at Birkenhead, Liverpool in 1958. He was a great character who enjoyed life to the full. We used to go to a posh pub in Thames Ditton where you would be certain to see a famous face from stage or screen. I retraced my steps years later to that same pub to see if anyone famous still enjoyed a drink there and I wasn't disappointed. I met actor William Hartnell, the original Dr Who.

Apart from our trips on the odd weekend and getting things in shape for the Gang Show, things were fairly ordinary. We were allowed to do as we wanted at Chessington and we were a self-contained unit. We slept in if we wanted and we had no parades. I remember a warrant officer bursting into our hut one day at about 9 a.m. We were all in bed. He flung open the door shouting, 'Everybody up.'

Tim Dormond's muffled voice came from under a blanket saying simply, 'Gang Shows.' All we heard next was the slamming of the door. We were called up to Cadogan Gardens to work on our wardrobe and, on arrival, we learned that the boss would be coming in. Squadron Leader Ralph Reader had been on a fact-finding tour of the Middle East, checking on his Gang Shows out there. As we waited to be taken into the wardrobe department, the main door opened and in walked the great man himself. I had only ever seen photographs of him, but photographs don't always do people justice. He had a powerful personality that hit you instantly. When he spoke, you paid attention.

'My God,' he fired out, slapping his hands all over his body, 'that sand gets everywhere.'

What a giant of a character Ralph Reader was. I can remember him shaking hands with everyone as he kept repeating: 'We gotta keep the boys happy, fellas. You're all doing a great job.' He then made his exit stage left, saying: 'Keep up the good work, fellas!'

While I was waiting my turn to be seen by the wardrobe 'mistress' –

who just happened to be a very tough-looking airman – Peter Sellers and I got the chance to chat. Peter told me he'd been surprised by the number of times my name had come up as having a similar act to his when he'd been in the officers' mess after his performances. We both laughed when I pointed out that I'd had to listen to talk of *him* doing an act like *mine*. It formed a bond between us right away. We chatted away, telling each other what our ambitions were in show business. Mine was to get more experience and work, but his was to break into films and Hollywood. I must admit that made me smile at the time. 'That'll be right,' I thought. A call from our wardrobe 'mistress' broke up our conversation.

Life was very busy. I had shows to do and I spent a lot of my spare time working in front of mirrors to try and improve my performing technique. I was writing my own comedy scripts and other comedy material that would be used by me in the future for broadcasting . . . Or so I hoped. Beryl and I were in contact a lot and I was slightly jealous of the fact that she had already been in the West End working at the Winter Garden Theatre in J.M. Barrie's *Peter Pan* as understudy to stage and movie star Ann Todd. That wonderful character-actor Alastair Sim was Captain Hook in that production and I still rate him as one of the very best actors in that role. And marriage remained on my mind. I still have my original RAF Conditions of Release and Authorisation Form that states I started with the princely sum of 3s 6d a day rising to 5s a day. Not a lot on which to contemplate a wedding and a life together. But I was still in my teens and the thought of money (or the lack of it) never entered my head.

We started to do shows at RAF camps all over the south of England. My stage work was getting better, and by watching and listening – and failing some of the time – I was learning to be a pro. For Christmas 1945 our small unit was told we had ten days' leave. It was a chance to make plans.

I had to break the news to Mum and Dad that I'd be going up north for Christmas. They showed no resentment and wished me luck. I was going to spend the festive season with Beryl and her family in their hometown of Bacup in Lancashire. Beryl's father, Fred, was a quarry owner who had several quarries around the county.

I think her family got a bit of a shock that their daughter was thinking of marrying a young man in the Air Force, not yet out of his teens, with no prospects and no money. I must have seemed a fair catch – if you wanted to commit hari-kari! I must say I was treated as if I was a sane and normal lad who just might have prospects. Not a word was said against our union and a date was set for our marriage.

Around this time Beryl was working in a revue for William Henshall – the man who discovered the late and great Sid Field (he was working for Henshall touring all the number-two theatres in the country as his principal comic when he was 'discovered', even though he'd been working in the business for years. Overnight he moved from £75 a week to £500 a week in a West End show in London). Beryl was touring and she knew she would have a break in April. I chanced my arm and thought I could get leave. So, we set the date for our wedding: 27 April 1946. After the Christmas period I returned to Gang Shows and Beryl continued touring in revue.

My life in the Gang Shows was never less than a thrill. Ralph Reader would have had around nine shows touring at any one time. I remember there was a lot of talk among the performers at the time about a chap called Dick Emery, another Gang Show member. He was making people in the world of show business sit up and take notice. People in entertainment always try to be one step ahead of the game and agents like Joe Collins (father of Joan Collins), among many others, knew that all the Gang Show talent was going to be demobbed in the near future. They were circling the talent like sharks. Talent is a funny thing. You have to have it. You can't make it. It's not something you can see. And sometimes it's hidden and it takes another talented person to spot it.

Stan Dale was one of those people. He could often see something no one else could in budding performers. A former air force man, for years after he was demobbed Stan wore his old RAF overcoat, and it earned him the nickname of Scruffy. Scruffy Dale went on to become one of the leading theatrical agents of his time.

I remember going to see Scruffy at his office in Regent Street after I left Gang Shows and being asked to wait there by the girl in the front office: first, because Scruffy wasn't in yet, and second, because there was someone else already waiting to see him. I looked at this other person and he was a dishevelled, shaggy-haired chap in a crumpled suit with a brown-paper parcel on his lap. After what seemed like ages, in walked Scruffy. I rose and said: 'I'm . . .'

And that's as far as I got. Holding his hand up he said to the other chap who'd been waiting for him to arrive: 'Sorry I'm late, come on.'

With that they both disappeared back down the stairs.

I asked the girl where they were going and how long I would have to wait for Scruffy's return. She shrugged her shoulders and returned to her typing. I waited nearly two hours in that office and then Scruffy Dale suddenly burst back through the door with a huge smile on his face.

'Some you win, some you lose,' he shouted. He looked at me and said, 'What are you waiting for? Come on in.'

I followed him into his office where he took off his trademark overcoat and tossed it onto a hat stand. I managed to tell him I was looking for a job when he told me I would have to do an audition for him just like the previous chap who'd been waiting in the office had done. He told me he'd taken the other wannabe down to a nearby audition room where he'd produced a pair of tap shoes out of his brown-paper parcel. He'd taken ages to put them on and then he performed a tap dance that was so bad it had to be seen to be believed. At the same time the man had never stopped apologising for how bad it all was and kept saying his aunt had kept him late, along with numerous other daft excuses.

Scruffy said it had been the most hilarious half-hour he'd ever spent. 'Today, my son, I have found a comedy star,' he told me.

I really wasn't all that interested. I wanted to talk about *me*.

'I've just come out of the Air Force,' I said, trying to interrupt his train of thought, 'and I'm a comedian.'

He jumped out of his seat and said: 'Maybe I've found TWO stars today. What's your name?'

'Glenn Buckland,' I replied.

'Good,' he said. 'I hope you're as good as that chap Frankie Howerd was today. He'll be a star. He was hilarious.'

And, of course, he was so right. Scruffy could see the raw talent behind all the fluffs and mistakes. He helped turn that unsure, crazy man into a star with a certain style.

As 1946 began all this was still ahead of me. By April of that year I had managed to get leave for my wedding. I arrived to discover a frightening request – the vicar wanted to see me. A time was arranged and I duly presented myself at the church to be met by a short, middle-aged man who sat me down and proceeded to tell me I should not be getting married.

'Do you know what you are letting yourself in for?' he inquired.

I said nothing.

'You're nineteen,' he said.

I said I would be twenty in May.

'All the same, marriage is a step you should give great thought to. I noticed him shaking his head ruefully as I left the room.

Three weeks after Beryl and I married, he ran away with his housekeeper . . .

The wedding went well. Mum and Dad arrived with a rather unusual wedding present – a 1937 Austin 7 that, as Dad announced proudly, had been owned by a pig farmer. He really didn't need to add this detail. You could smell the car before you saw it. He meant well but it fell apart weeks after our wedding . . .

The ceremony itself was mobbed by fans who knew Beryl, and at the reception I made a memorable groom's speech. This was not so much because of what I said, perhaps, but rather because of the surprise appearance of one of my socks. In order to give my jacket a fashionable square-shouldered look, I had stuffed a sock under each shoulder to pad it out. But unfortunately, as I leant forward at one stage, the motion caused one of the socks to ping out, landing on the white tablecloth, in full view of the whole wedding party. Having no alternative, I had to make the best of it, so making a joke of the matter, I hastily stuffed the sock back in place to counter my now comically lopsided appearance.

We were woken the next morning by a knock at the door as a Sunday paper was slipped into our room. There were three weddings on the front page and we were one of the couples. Written on the newspaper was what we thought was a bit of a cheeky message: 'Good morning, sir, we hope you had a pleasant night!'

We spent our honeymoon in London in a bed and breakfast in Brixton, taking a room that had a huge brass bed. It wasn't far from the old Brixton Empire, a great variety theatre in those days.

I can recall seeing Benny Hill in a double act with Joe Baker there. They did a musical tennis act. They never spoke and did the whole thing in fluorescent lighting with a blackout stage. Benny and Joe were dressed in black and each held a fluorescent tennis racket to play their game. Their fluorescent ball did somersaults and all manner of crazy things as they 'hit' it backwards and forwards over the imaginary net. The crazy-ball antics were carried out by a third man dressed in black who was actually holding it as the comics pretended to hit it back and forth. It doesn't sound very funny written down like this and it was even worse when you saw it. That was in the days when Benny Hill was only doing bits and pieces such as acting as a 'feed' (straight man) for comics. He certainly wasn't famous back then. In fact his partner in that awful tennis act was a comic. Joe Baker went on to become quite a big theatrical agent. I think audiences had a lucky escape!

Our honeymoon turned into a 'looking for work' week. It ended with Beryl getting a new manager – Jimmy Retford – brother of the famous music-hall star Ella Retford. It wasn't long before she was off in another one of the William Henshall revues. And I returned to the Gang Shows, entertaining at RAF Camps here, there and everywhere.

12

Eastern entertaining

In July 1946 I got the call. Tim, who was in charge of my Gang Show unit, was summoned to London. He came back from Cadogan Gardens looking very pleased with himself. Tim had been talking to Ralph; it seemed that my unit was going on tour to the Far East in August. For how long we didn't know or really care. We were off to see the world.

It took some time for us to be kitted out with all our gear for the tropics. We had to carry our own mosquito nets and I was going back into short trousers. When we were done we stood looking at ourselves in the mirror – we could have been an early prototype for the cast of *It Ain't Half Hot, Mum*.

We set off from RAF Lyneham on 1 August 1946 in a twin-engine Dakota bound for Cairo. We were staying at the Heliopolis Palace, a magnificent luxury hotel. After we arrived, I couldn't wait to get my sticky, sweaty shirt off and get into the pool. I had been warned about the fierceness of the sun but I took no notice and only five minutes later started to feel the pain. I was yelling in agony and had never felt anything like it. It was searing. I soon learned to keep my skin protected from the sun. But there was no protection from the kids in the street who would follow you for hours with cries of 'Shoe shine! Shoe shine!' If you didn't stop to get one, they'd splash you and your shoes with red paint. One day I stopped at the gates of the hotel after a visit to the bazaar. 'OK,' I said.

Big mistake.

I was engulfed by children trying to attend to my feet. Watched by a fair crowd of Egyptians, I put my hand in my pocket to pay them to find I had only one halfpenny in English money. I gave it to a boy with his hand thrust out in front of me. The boy looked at it and then began yelling blue murder. Everyone in the crowd took up the cry. I didn't know what they were saying and I had no intention of staying to find out. I made my escape from the crowd and the army guards at the entrance to the hotel had to force the gates shut.

I'll always remember my first morning in Cairo. I was woken from an exhausted sleep by what I thought, at the time, was the sound of millions of bees buzzing. After struggling out of my mosquito net I made my way to the window. Dawn was just coming up. I looked out from the hotel onto the desert and all I could see was a huge cloud of dust coming my way. At first I thought it was a sandstorm, and then I could see it was hundreds of people shuffling along in their sandals (this was the strange sound of buzzing I'd heard), all making their way into the city to start work. It was like a scene from *Lawrence of Arabia* – all that was missing was the sweeping orchestral score.

We only had a few days in Cairo then it was on to Rangoon by plane – just a bare cylinder shell with the odd seat along each side of the fuselage. The wartime airstrips were not much better, being made up of metal sheets laid end to end. When we touched down the wheels made a noise as if the aircraft was breaking up. We had to come into Burma over trees and get down quickly because the metal runway was a very short cleaning in the jungle. We sang our signature tune, 'Crest of a Wave', as we came in to land. We were given native huts as our living quarters and they were dotted around the airfield. There were no barriers or anything like that to guard the airfield – or us, for that matter.

We were told that we had to watch out for bandits, who had a habit of sneaking into the native huts, which had no doors or windows, and stealing anything they could lay their hands on. After this warning we were allocated our accommodation, two to a hut. Tim Dormond was in with me and he pinched the camp bed in the far corner of the hut. The only other bed was right at the open doorway. We had been told the bandits carried machetes and if they thought that you might interfere with their pilfering they wouldn't hesitate to use their weapons on you. We were also told: 'Don't put your bed near the open doorway. They'll slit your throat first then steal anything after that.'

When I look back on those times I can remember Tim sometimes being a little under the weather, probably caused by a bit of alcoholic over-indulgence. I used to have the odd glass of beer to keep him company, and one particular night we had been drinking and chatting with some of the RAF boys on the airstrip and were making our way back to our hut.

Unfortunately, it was the monsoon season. I have never seen rain like it – it didn't come down in sheets, it came down along with the bed as well! I was trying to hold on to Tim to steady him, and maybe that's how it all happened. The first I knew of the danger was when I started to fall. As I staggered to my feet seconds later I found to my horror that we had walked straight into a monsoon trench which had been dug to catch the heavy rainfall. I was soaking wet, and no doubt Tim was in an even worse condition, as he was still lying in a heap in the bottom of the trench. But actually he probably wasn't in a fit state to feel anything: he was out cold.

It was only when I looked up that the panic set in. The trench we had fallen into was about six feet deep and the rain was filling it up fast. I tried climbing up the side, but to no avail, as every foothold I gained I immediately lost again as the earth crumbled away and I fell crashing back down. The water was rising terrifyingly fast. Thankfully I managed to waken Tim out of his drunken slumber and hauled him to his feet and he too made desperate attempts to climb out. No use. Still the water was rising, and by this stage we could hardly stand up as it was rushing downhill into the trench so fast.

117

I have never seen a drunken man sober up more quickly than my mate Tim.

'If we don't get out, we're going to drown,' he yelled above the sound of the rushing water. To put it mildly, I agreed with him.

We both began to yell at the tops of our voices as the water crept ever higher and higher. But just then another problem then popped into my head to add to our worries. 'I can't swim!' I screamed out.

Tim, the athlete, stared at me with wet, bloodshot eyes. 'Neither can I!' he screamed back at me.

We redoubled our efforts. We were so lucky, as another couple of chaps, who'd been having a drink or two, heard our shouts. With the help of some rope they helped us to clamber out of our watery tomb.

As I said I have never seen anyone sober up so fast in my life. I don't remember seeing Tim take another drink after that escapade. Of course, I continued enjoying the odd half pint!

Everything was very primitive out in the Far East. God knows what it must have been like when the fighting was going on. It was bad enough for us trying to get from RAF camp to RAF camp to entertain the boys.

Our itinerary called for us to do shows in the areas around Rangoon, Calcutta, Karachi and Singapore. At one time we did a stop-over in Bangkok where I got the shock of my life. Some RAF guys took us to a Bangkok nightclub; after a few drinks I decided to go to the toilet. I was minding my own business when two or three local ladies appeared in the gents' toilet. I was shocked and made a quick exit. When I told my friends of this unnerving experience everyone roared with laughter.

'That's the way it is all the time here,' they said.

It was on our trip to Karachi that I met many of the other show stars who were working out there. We sometimes used to travel in open trucks and on one occasion on our way to do a show from our base in Karachi we had engine trouble. An open truck coming the other way stopped and asked our driver if he wanted any help. I idly wandered to the back of their truck and saw a bunch of chaps in army uniforms huddled together.

A/C Buckland – 18 years old.

Trying to look like a serious actor.

Bernard Lee, left, Glenn Buckland, and Jennifer Jayne in a scene from the award-winning film *The Blue Lamp*.

RIGHT. My father looking bemused at Yonnie's wedding. This was his 'Will that be all, my Lady?' look.

BELOW. No, I wasn't showing Beryl who was boss! She had confetti in her eye and I was attempting to get it out.

My daughter Yonnie's after-christening party. Far left are Beryl's mum and dad and, far right, my mum and dad.

Beryl at her dressing table, Palace Theatre, Manchester for the panto *Humpty Dumpty*.

RIGHT. I look a bit nervous at the prospect of fatherhood!

BELOW. Beryl as Principal Boy in panto at the Hippodrome, Stockport.

BOTTOM. Beryl, Yonnie and me in Granny's back garden in Bacup.

LEFT. Me trying to look relaxed in Banchory on a day out.

BELOW. The Gaiety Whirl, Ayr, 1958. I'm centre stage, Jack Milroy has a girl on his knee. On the right are The Four Ramblers, who included Val Doonican (back row, third from the right).

Stepps, Glasgow. Young Chris tries to tow our caravan. Some hope!

I was never any good at DIY, as this picture of my garage in Prestwick in the 60s clearly shows. Chris 'helps' me.

ABOVE. I'm doing an outside broadcast for STV interviewing Walter McGowan WBC flyweight champion, 1966. (STV)

LEFT. Rikki Fulton and me in a radio-type show for TV, one of Rikki's many ideas.

ABOVE. Here I'm a bumbling professor in a Francie and Josie TV Show called 'The Volunteers'. (STV)

RIGHT. A Francie and Josie episode with me as a very nasty Arab. This picture was taken after the show. It was so hot in the studio I was only just hanging onto my false nose and beard. (STV)

Francie and Josie again. Rehearsal time, so Jack left his trademark wig off. (STV)

Rehearsal time again, this time for *The Rikki Fulton Hour* with me, second left, Rikki, centre, Ethel Scott, second right, and the wonderful Duncan Macrae, far right. (STV)

Rikki and me with Clem Ashby, right. Jack Milroy had suddenly been taken ill and I took over as Josie's cousin. A TV first! (STV)

Another Francie and Josie episode: Rikki and Jack with me as the silly-ass officer. (STV)

'The Haunted House' – a Francie and Josie episode for STV where I was a wicked old fool who scared the living daylights out of both of them. (STV)

The boys as city gents and me as 'M'. (STV)

Another *Rikki Fulton Hour* with me, centre left with Rikki, Clem Ashby, between us, and Walter Jackson and Ethel Scott, Rikki's first wife. (STV)

I'm the Old Time Chairman of the One o'Clock Gang's Music Hall here with Dorothy Paul, her usual charming self. (STV)

On location with Rikki in Crail, Fife, for 'The Grand Tour', supposedly set in Yugoslavia. I'm the one in the hat. (STV)

A madcap scene from Una McLean's TV series *Over to Una*, with Effie Morrison, Una, me and Phil McCall. (STV)

The *Over to Una* TV series with Una and me as arguing brother and sister. (STV)

Jimmy Logan and me in 'Friends and Neighbours' (1965), a special TV production of *The Jimmy Logan Theatre Hour*. (STV)

Same show – I'm horsing around on the sofa with Walter Carr and Jimmy, who is hidden by me. (STV)

For STV Plays on the telly – me doing my nut in *The Silver Soldier* in 1966. (STV)

One of many outfits I wore for a series of fun TV captions – an idea by great director Bryan Izzard. (STV)

Presenting a programme for STV called *Would You Believe It?*, a network show in the late '70s. (STV)

More presenting, this time *Search for Beauty*. Looking for talent. Nothing changes. (STV)

Making a quick getaway from STV's studios in Cowcaddens. Rusty leads the way. (STV)

An early picture of Rudi and Rusty getting a titbit. (STV)

LEFT. The husky voice of Rusty – or so you might think. Wrong. He was smiling at me to get a treat. (STV)

BELOW. The film of Walt Disney's *The Aristocats* was a big success in 1970, and here they are, larger than life with me in the studio for a *Cavalcade* show. (STV)

RIGHT. My favourite photo of Rusty (2) as a young puppy. What a cracker he was. (STV)

Another favourite photo: a Christmas *Cavalcade* in 1970. Joining me in the studio were daughter Yonnie and son Chris and, I nearly forgot, Rudi! (STV)

An early picture of me pinning up some 'Letters of the Month' on the *Cavalcade* board. (STV)

I'm getting set upon by pop band Slick, my guests on *Cavalcade*. Can you spot Midge Ure? He's second on the left. (STV)

Monkey business from Calderpark Zoo's Richard O'Grady. (STV)

Me with some more Disney characters, this time from *Robin Hood,* disrupt Sauchiehall Street, Glasgow, before a TV show in 1973. (STV)

Yours truly with my 1975 award for 'Best ITV programme'. I still have the trousers, though they don't fit now! (STV)

Wedding day for Yonnie and her husband, Colin McInnes. A toast from us all in Ayr's Western House.

My son Chris and his lovely new wife, Anne, being ignored by the terrible trio – Jack, Rikki and me. Anything for a laugh!

ABOVE. Spot the Santa wandering through Turnberry Hotel's plush kitchens. The things I do for my art!

LEFT. An Easter parade starring Kenny Dalglish and Co.

One of my children's Christmas parties in the STV Studios. (STV)

Just an excuse to get Paladin the Lamp and Totty the Robot into the Christmas spirit. Ha! ha! (STV)

Paladin had helped this little boy get better after being ill in Yorkhill Hospital, Glasgow. He was a real TV star. (STV)

A young visitor to *Cavalcade* presenting me with a 'Happy Laugher Award'. A surprise live event from the Dennistoun Festival of 1981. (STV)

One of many visits to Edinburgh Zoo.

Two famous football names and me at Edinburgh Castle for a special party.
Turn the book upside down to find the answer.

Terry Butcher and Andy Roxburgh.

LEFT. One of many photoshoots featuring Bugs Bunny.

BELOW. A very special photograph taken at Fraser's store in Glasgow, our Christmas home for many years in the mid 80s. My son Chris, grandson Grant and myself after one of my live shows in the specially constructed Fraser's theatre.

RIGHT. Youngest grandson Mark Buckland, all grown up.

BELOW LEFT. Me, Beryl, grandson Mark and canine star Rusty.

BELOW RIGHT. Grandsons Grant, left, and Fraser McInnes, Christmas 2007.

The first to speak was a round-faced guy with a pleasant grin.

'Hello, where are you going, then?' he enquired.

I said we were RAF Gang Shows and we were going to do a show. All the faces looked down at me as he said, laughing, 'We're Stars in Battledress. I'm Arthur Haynes.' (He later became a big comedian on stage and television.)

Another face appeared behind him.

'I'm the sergeant in charge of this mob,' he said and stretched out his hand over the tailboard. As I shook it he continued, 'Charlie Chester's the name.'

He proceeded to introduce the other members of his band of entertainers: first, Ken Morris, and then, tucked up in the corner of the truck I got a 'before-it-was-famous' toothy grin from England's most notorious cad, Terry-Thomas. The names meant nothing to me then; they were just a bunch of guys doing a bit of entertaining. Charlie Chester was to become a national institution with his radio shows like *Stand Easy* and *Sunday Soapbox*, which both ran for over twenty years, while Arthur Haynes and Ken Morris were members of his radio company for many years.

After doing many shows in all sorts of venues, we headed for Singapore in October. We were greeted by a wonderful climate and a very gentle people. We were stationed near the notorious Changi jail. There were Japanese soldiers, still in uniform, absolutely everywhere, mostly in working parties doing all sorts of jobs like cleaning the streets and loading and unloading British and American trucks. As we drove through the streets we noticed that if the Japanese saw you and you saw them they had to stop what they were doing and bow or salute you. It all felt very strange.

We did many shows to very good audiences until the word came that we were going home. We were told we could go back to the UK in one of two ways – by boat, which would take a few weeks, or we could fly back over seven days in one of the twin-engine Dakotas that was going home to be broken up for scrap. The officer who told us this said it with

119

a smile and added: 'You can go and see it if you like. It's on the runway. Oh, and by the way, it's number 13 and painted green.'

He might have thought this was funny, but to me it was a nightmare. I decided to go and see it for myself because we all wanted to get home as soon as we could, but safely. When I saw it I nearly died of shock. It looked like a lame duck, and was leaning to one side with a flat tyre. I had a huge desire to cry. There was a guy in overalls fussing around it. It turned out that he was a warrant officer who, in fact, would be the pilot flying the plane home to the UK. I reported these disturbing findings to Tim and the rest of the unit and we decided we'd take the risk and fly home. The day we set off was a day I will never forget.

We all arrived to board our Dakota aircraft at the appointed time. There was no farewell party or departure lounge. We just walked out to the plane and there it was, waiting to be taken to the scrap heap. The pilot's crew looked to be in a good mood, because I suppose, they were going home. We all got settled in the aircraft and the engines started up. If you wanted to talk you had to shout above the engine noise. We started to move forward and up to the end of the runway where we turned, ready for take-off.

Now, you were supposed to warm the engine up so that it didn't stall on take-off. Our pilot didn't think this was necessary and yelled back to us: 'Hold tight.' At this point we all fell to the back of the plane from where we had been sitting as we had no belts to hold us in. The noise was horrendous. We were being shaken out of our skins as our pilot sent the aircraft tearing down the short runway. He was whooping and singing and I suddenly felt as if my stomach had dropped into my boots as we took off in a steep climb. Our tangled bundle of frightened human flesh cowered at the back of the plane. As we levelled out I heard the engine noise settle down to a thunderous shaking, rather like the sound of some giant washing machine about to conk out. The voice of our crazy pilot came back to us.

'We made it!' he yelled, and this statement was followed by a rather high-pitched laugh. 'If you want to come up front, feel free.' I gathered myself together because no one else wanted to take up his offer and staggered forward to the cockpit.

It was then that I saw it. You've heard of having a 'monkey on your back'. Well, our pilot was going one better. He had a real live monkey perched on his joystick. 'I call him Joey. He's a bit of a clown,' he shouted at me. Very original, I thought. At that moment jumped up and made a frantic tour of the cockpit swinging from anything it could grab hold of – including my hair – before going back to sit on our pilot's lap, where it received murmurs of affection from its master. When we stopped in Malta on our seven-day trip back to the UK, the little fellow died. The change in temperature was too much for him.

I remember waking up in the middle of the night on Flight 13 Green. I had been dozing on and off when something about the movement of the aircraft told me we were in a bit of bother. It was rocking from side to side; looking out of a small porthole-sized window, I got the shock of my life. We were flying low over mountainous seas. I could see the white crests of the waves – we were as close to the sea as that. The pilot was struggling hard to control the Dakota. Everyone was awake now – and scared. I staggered up to the cockpit and asked if we were in trouble

'You could say that,' came the reply. 'We've hit a bad storm and I can't get above it so I've had to try to get under it. That means flying about a hundred feet above the sea. So you'd better tell everyone to sit tight and pray.'

We did exactly that for what seemed like ages. It was due to his magnificent flying ability that we came through. At the end of the journey home I realised I was sad to leave the old aircraft behind, knowing it was going to be broken up. All of us felt the same. We were also aware of what it represented: our Gang Show days were numbered. Things were going to change, and we would have to change as well.

13

Back in Britain

On our return we all gathered at Cadogan Gardens, Gang Show HQ, if you recall, and I was sent to a billet in St John's Wood called Viceroy Court. The particular rooms in my section of the building happened to look onto the back of other flats occupied by the civilian population. After being there a short time I noticed that there were always people at the windows of those flats looking over at us, and as the days passed it gradually dawned on me (being a young lad with a sharp eye) that the window watchers were all teenage girls.

Now, our windows were without curtains and at night the lights were on full pelt, so there was nothing to stop anyone from seeing us doing whatever it was we happened to be doing. And indeed, during the evenings, the girls seemed to stare even more intently. I decided to investigate.

One night after dark I found my way to a vantage point on the ground between both buildings. To the left I could see the five storeys of our RAF billets, the curtainless windows lit up like a stage. To my right was the other building, with its audience of girls at almost every window, waving and jumping about trying to draw attention to themselves. Word must have got round to every girl in the neighbourhood that the RAF were in town. So there we were, just like in Army camps, providing entertainment. Though what type of entertainment our boys in blue were putting on to elicit such an excited response – well, I couldn't possibly comment!

Despite our nightly audience of admirers, my time at Viceroy Court was spent mostly waiting around kicking my heels. Gang Shows were winding down fast by now and Peter Sellers had told me he was spending his days off trying to look for other openings. I thought I should be doing the same but, unlike Peter, I had no clue as to how to go about it. I was told by the powers that be: 'Keep your head down and wait for the call.'

Christmas was upon us, it would soon be 1947, and I was due to be demobbed in April.

I got leave and set off for Manchester – Beryl was appearing in pantomime with an all-star cast in *Humpty Dumpty* at the Palace Theatre. The stars were Jimmy James as the king (for my money the funniest man ever to grace a stage) and the dame was the very West End style of performer, and big star of his day, Arthur Riscoe. Beryl was understudy to principal girl Mary Naylor. When she became ill one night Beryl made a great success of taking over her part, creating quite a stir. The show was produced by the London Palladium producer Robert Nisbet and its run lasted from November right through to March (as pantomimes did in those days).

I arrived just too late to see Beryl getting her big chance. But as I reached the stage door in my RAF uniform I was greeted by two zany comedians, Syd and Max Harrison, who pushed me into Jimmy James' dressing room. Jimmy promptly greeted me as if I'd won the war. He plied me with drink and loads of goodies. Pros are like that. They are the warmest, most kind-hearted people you'll ever meet in life. I was delighted for Beryl because it was one of the best pantomimes I'd ever seen – full of comedy and spectacle.

My leave over, the demobbing call came. I had to report to Padgate, the same station I had joined up at. When I arrived it was a madhouse. Some people were coming, some were going. There were forms to fill in, uniforms to be handed in, and my demob suit to get, along with a hat, shirt, tie and shoes. I thought it would be a good idea if I picked a suit that others didn't have. I could see three others in front of me picking a sports jacket and trousers so I thought I'd go for a natty, striped, bright blue, serge suit and a blue trilby hat with black shoes. You were allowed to try your outfit on and I opted to keep it all on. I was so glad to be out of my uniform. I practically ran out of RAF Padgate and made my way to the station. As I waited for the train to London I looked along the platform. There was a mass of humanity waiting for the train to a new life. It was a picture to behold. Every man was wearing the same suit as mine. Same hat, same shoes. It would have been a producer's dream for a production number in a musical film (call it 'The Men in the Blue Serge Suits'). I nearly died of embarrassment, along with about a hundred others on that platform.

When the train finally came we all tried to get away from each other but there was nowhere to go. Our arrival in London was the same with everyone trying to get out of each other's way. You could hear the laughter, not from any of us, but from the people we had to face in that long walk up the platform and through the station.

I had saved a little money, and as Beryl was touring in revue I took the chance to see my parents who, by this time, had moved yet again. This time they had obtained a position in Newmarket. They had a nice house and I was offered a settee to sleep on while I was there. Dad asked me what I was going to do and I told him I was going to try to break into films. He said I should have my own transport and he knew a man who knew a man who could sell me an MG Sports for £55. I met the guy with the car and had a trial run – it seemed to drive well enough. I paid my £55 to him in cash and away he walked. I felt this was a new start for me. Out of the RAF and a car of my own – and an MG Sports no less. I was going up in the world.

My first trip in the car was to the bookies to back a horse that lost its race. I also lost my car. I came out of the bookies and set off; as I changed gear there was a sickening crunch and the car stopped, never to start again. The garage showed me the car up on a ramp. I saw there were four-inch nails driven into the clutch plate to keep it together. The list of other faults was endless. So, the car was a write-off . . . I left it with the garage for scrap. Not the most auspicious of beginnings to the next chapter in my life . . .

Beryl was at the Oldham Empire and I arrived after one of the worst falls of snow ever. People still talk about the winter of 1947. I knocked on the door of the address she had given me and it was opened by a thick-set guy in a see-through, sleeveless vest, short trousers, a ten-day growth of beard and a face like an all-in wrestler. By the smell him, I suspected his wrestling partner might well have been a whisky bottle. I asked if my wife was staying there to be told that she was and he showed me to her room on the ground floor. I opened the door to discover Beryl lying on a mattress that was covered over by a bundle of clothes. The room was filthy and as cold as ice. I told her to pack; she wasn't staying in this dump a moment longer.

We left without paying and found new digs. I saw the show a couple of times and then returned to London to look for work. Beryl was ending her revue tour soon, so I found a flat in Kensington that was reasonable to rent, although it had no phone. Everyone used the phone on the landing every time it rang twenty people dashed to answer it. It would have worked out just fine if the other nineteen hadn't been prostitutes. Many a time I would run for the phone and a voice would ask: 'Is that Rosa? Are you busy?'

'She's not here, she must be—' I'd begin, and then put the phone down.

At this time I had registered with a film-casting agency. You would call at their offices in Denmark Street in the afternoon to see if there was any work for you the following day as an extra, or, if you were really lucky, a few lines in a film. I was sent many times to Denham Studios, Elstree, Isleworth, and other studios of the day. Sometimes I would get the odd line to say. If the director picked you, of course, you'd get extra money.

The first film I did was at Elstree. They wanted people for a café scene in one of David Farrar's films. He was a big number-two star in those days.

I can't remember the title of the film but I recall sitting along with a few others pretending to eat and drink. I was at a table with a very elderly gentleman who was very pleasant and smiled at everything that was going on. He was just one of the crowd. I was later told that I'd been sitting with one of the most famous music-hall comedians of all time – George Roby. They called him the 'Prime Minister of Mirth' and he was a legend of the theatre.

I was earning at last. I managed to get a few speaking lines in a film to be shot in Isleworth. I had been recommended by a director to the casting agency as 'having potential'. The film was directed by Commander Anthony Kimmins, a very well-known director and a personal friend of the Royal family. In the 1930s he'd directed Googie Withers and the future *My Fair Lady* star Rex Harrison in a film called *All at Sea* for the great Alexander Korda. This was to be another Korda film, called *Mine Own Executioner* and taken from the book by Nigel Balchin. Its lead actors were Kieron Moore, Christine Norden (a new recruit) and Dulcie Gray, whose husband was that fine actor Michael Denison. But the real star of the film was the American actor Burgess Meredith who, like so many other Americans, had arrived to make films in Britain because of the lack of work in the US.

I had a few lines in the bar where Burgess Meredith and Christine Norden were drinking. I was a barman and I had to ask them if they would like another drink. I rehearsed my lines over and over again in the toilet to make sure I didn't fluff them. I made so many trips to the toilet people must have thought I was suffering from diarrhoea. It was the only place I could find to go over my script in peace.

Quite a lot of action took place in the bar between Meredith and Norden, who was a lovely blonde lady. She had to keep fighting off Burgess's attention, but not during the film action – it was when we stopped filming that she had this particular problem.

He had a tremendous sense of fun. To Meredith, acting was a game to be enjoyed. When the cameras rolled he was the true professional and never forgot his lines. When filming was over he always wanted to have a

127

laugh and would play little tricks on anyone who happened to be near him after a scene was shot. I remember he asked Christine to rehearse a closer cuddle with him at the bar. He said it would make the scene more powerful. She agreed and he then proceeded to tickle her until she fell off the stool with Burgess ending up on the floor too, roaring with laughter. I think it was his way of getting through the long days of filming.

The studios at Iselworth were a bit dreary. In years gone by it had actually been Worton Hall – a big country mansion in magnificent grounds near Hounslow. There were wooded glades and huge lawns and terraces that could be used for exterior filming, but it was a shadow of its former self in 1947. However, I remember I arrived for my fourth day of filming to be greeted by an incredible sight. When I had left filming the day before, the entrance – a long driveway – had been completely, and starkly, bare. Now there was a tree-lined avenue with lawns and flowerbeds. There were gangs of men erecting streetlamps and flags. I asked one of the men working on the newly placed turf what was happening. He told me he didn't know. I got the same answer from the wardrobe department, the sound department and the clapper boy (although he did give me one titbit of information: 'It's a secret,' he said with a grin). I was still trying to find out what this was all about when I spotted Leslie Mitchell from British Movietone News – for so many years the friendly voice of world news in the cinema when I was growing up. I pretended to cross his path and as I did so I said, 'Big change, eh?'

'Big visitors,' he said, smiling as he walked on.

I still didn't know what was going on, but there was a clue at least.

When I got onto the set, ready for filming, Anthony Kimmins was waiting there along with Burgess, Christine, Keiron and Dulcie. The only other person called that day was me. Commander Kimmins began speaking to the assembled cast just as I walked in.

'So, I hope you don't mind playing along? It'll take some time but we'll catch up later.' He ushered the four stars into a line, then spotting me, he said, 'You might as well join them. It looks a bigger company.'

I was still in the dark as to what this was all about when Burgess Meredith raised his arms in the air and shouted at the top of his voice, 'Bring on the royals!'

It would have been about 11 a.m. and we had been there since 8 a.m. I had done no filming at all and had just sat in the corner watching the others rehearse. The director was away meeting whomever it was who was coming so Burgess had plenty of time to act out his jokes on those who would put up with them.

Leslie Mitchell suddenly burst onto the set and told us to get in line – quickly. Everyone dashed to his or her appointed positions, including me on the end. The studio crew stopped talking and playing cards. Silence descended as Commander Anthony Kimmins ushered into the studio Her Royal Highness Princess Elizabeth and Her Royal Highness Princess Margaret. I nearly fainted.

Commander Kimmins started to introduce the line-up to the princesses. He explained who everyone was and what he or she was doing in the film. It was a case of shaking hands, smiling, and moving on. Everything was going to plan until the royal party came to Burgess – the star who in future years would play the Penguin in the TV series of *Batman*. I think he must have been rehearsing for this moment, because, as he shook hands, he did a delightful curtsey, smiled, and said, 'Hi, Princess.'

Anthony Kimmins drew a breath, Princess Elizabeth smiled, Princess Margaret giggled and I nearly died of shock. I was next in line to shake hands. I think it must have thrown Kimmins a bit because he turned to move the party on when Princess Elizabeth held out her hand to me. I shook it gently and she smiled at me.

'He plays the waiter,' the director said.

No name, no nothing – just 'the waiter'.

They had two chairs for the royal party and they sat facing the set. Commander Kimmins explained to the princess that he was going to shoot a scene and asked if they would like to watch. They said they'd be delighted and Burgess Meredith and Christine Norden were set up at the bar for their scene. Thank goodness this scene didn't involve me. I sat out of sight to watch. They did their scene and the director called out 'Cut' to end the filming.

There was a polite round of applause interrupted by Burgess who said, in an extremely loud voice, directly addressing the princesses, 'You do know there was no film in the camera? Cheat, eh?' The royal party smiled and the director gave Burgess a look that could have killed at ten paces. Burgess added to his fun by shrugging his shoulders, 'So? We don't have royals in the US.'

Leslie Mitchell was hovering in the background and I think he'd decided enough was enough. We were herded towards the exit and outside there was a beautiful limousine waiting for the two princesses.

Everyone who had worked on the film, and it was a fair-sized crowd, had gathered to give them a send-off. Burgess Meredith decided to take charge of the proceedings to show that America supported the Royal family. As the two princesses were about to get into their car Princess Margaret turned to give a dazzling smile, almost a wink, to the handsome Kieron Moore, who was standing with everyone else in the crowd to say farewell. Burgess raised his arms high in the air and yelled, 'Three cheers for Princess Elizabeth.'

We all duly obliged.

'Three cheers for Princess Margaret,' he continued.

Again we cheered but with more vigour this time. The door of the limousine was being held open by a well-dressed chauffeur who was standing to attention with eyes front.

'And now,' said Burgess. 'Let's hear three cheers for the chauffeur!' There was utter silence – apart from the distinct sound of choking coming from Anthony Kimmins, who was perhaps visualising his head on the block at the Tower of London. And in the end I faced my own version of the chop – all my scenes in the making of *Mine Own Executioner* ended up on the cutting-room floor.

I continued trying to get bigger parts but my only claim to fame in those days was that I never had to do another job outside of acting to support myself. I never washed up, served at tables, or begged for a crust. Throughout my entire career I have always worked in my chosen profession.

That year, 1948, was hard going. I bumped into Peter Sellers outside my old haunt, the Express Dairy in Charing Cross Road, and he told me he was looking for work. I told him I was finding it hard to get anything other than walk-ons, bit-parts, and work as an extra. I said that if things didn't get a bit better I was heading for the variety theatres of the north.

Peter threw his hands in the air.

'Don't leave London,' he said. 'You'll never get back in. I don't care what happens, I'm staying until I get something.'

He did, of course, get something.

The next time I saw him he was bottom of the bill at the London Palladium – but that was like being top of the bill at any other theatre. I admit I was envious; I knew I had to find work.

Beryl was performing in a succession of revues and was doing well. When she was free we did a double act of comedy and song. We played anywhere and everywhere. I remember playing the Grand Theatre, Byker, in Newcastle, for Beryl's old boss William Henshall. We got the fright of our lives when we discovered the wire netting over the orchestra pit. The stage manager told us on the Monday before we opened: 'Friday nights, they get a bit noisy, son.' He was right. They threw steel rivets at the performers they didn't like . . . (The wire netting was to protect the orchestra – regardless of the standard of the performers, they were blameless.)

We were lucky. They liked us and we just got laughs. Our double act did very well in most theatres. Those were the days when, if you were an act, you had to submit a script to the Lord Chamberlain who would look at it to make sure there was nothing inappropriate in it and then give you approval to perform.

I once submitted a script in which I said to a bus driver at a bus stop:

'Do you go to Salford?'

'No,' he said.

'Well, it says Salford on the front,' I retorted.

'It says Epsom Salts on the back but I don't take 'em,' he shot back.

The Lord Chamberlain's office put a red line through that one as it was considered to be lavatorial patter . . .

The local Watch Committee would sit in the front stalls of theatre with a copy of your script. If you deviated from it, you didn't play the second house. Today's comedians with their frequent use of the F-word and other observations on sex would have given the Watch Committee members heart attacks.

Beryl and I decided we would put on a touring revue. We got a string of dates for the number-two theatres in towns like Ashton-under-Lyne, Bilston, Islington, Bishop Auckland and Loughborough, the last of which proved to be a problem for us.

Top of our bill was an act called Wheeler and Wilson, a father and son; they were billed as 'The Sailor and the Porter'. Jimmy Wheeler, the son, became famous on radio and the music hall with his catchphrase, 'Aye, aye, that's yer lot,' at the end of his act.

We arrived in the fair city of Loughborough, a university town, all ready to open. We were doing our band call with the orchestra when the manager came up to me.

'Where's your nude?' he asked.

Slightly taken aback, I asked him to repeat the question.

'Oh aye, every show that comes 'ere has a nude.'

I informed him, loftily, that ours was a family show. We had never, ever, had any nudes.

'No nude, no show,' he stated with conviction, and off he walked.

A conversation with the stage manager settled the matter. We had to have a nude in the show because the students of Loughborough demanded it as their right. We had a chorus line-up in the show of eight young ladies, all delightful girls looking for fame and a start in show business. I had a word with Beryl and we decided the only thing to do was talk to the girls. I tapped on their dressing-room door and was invited in. The request that followed was taken in by eight, decent-living, young ladies.

'I need a nude.'

Gasps and giggles followed by a deafening silence.

'Girls, I'm sorry to do this to you but we have to have a nude in the show or we can't open. Is anyone willing to do a nude for me?' I pleaded. 'There's an extra ten shillings in it for you at the end of the week.'

Once again, silence. Then a small, timid voice said, 'I'll do it.'

There were more gasps and looks of horror from the other seven girls.

'I'll do it on one condition. My mum must never know,' said our saviour.

'Don't worry, I have an idea,' I told her.

We had a scene where the girls danced in a woodland setting (well, a backcloth with trees on it). We had one freestanding tree in the middle of the stage that the girls danced around to the music of the Sugar Plum Fairy. We opened on time, having assured the manager we did indeed now have a nude scene and everything was going well. In the second half our Sugar Plum Fairy scene music played and our dancers performed to increasingly voluble cries of, 'Shame,' and boos from the audience.

They had spotted my nude – and they didn't like it. I had positioned my timid young nude behind the tree and all you could see of her from the front of the house was one arm sticking out of the trunk, one leg and a smiling face leaning out from behind the tree.

The important point was, we had a nude – and we could play the week out. Miss Timid got her ten shillings and we *never* told her mum. We also never played Loughborough again . . .

For those who are aspiring to make a name in show business, let me give a word of warning. If you get an inflated idea of yourself it's sometimes a good idea for something, or somebody, to bring you down to earth. Musicians are the greatest at doing this as I found out.

When Beryl and I did our double act of comedy and singing we thought we were doing rather well for a young couple in our twenties. We were going to all sorts of theatres and the reception of our act was excellent.

One week we finished a show on the Saturday night and travelled by train to Middlesbrough as we were playing the Empire there. They had a nice orchestra of about twelve musicians. We put our band parts down on the Monday morning on stage, as near to the centre as we could get. The reason for doing that is it's the tradition of Variety that when you arrive in a theatre you take your 'band call' – a run-through with the band – so you don't muck it all up on the Monday night. You place your band parts in a line from the centre stage in order of arrival at the theatre. If someone had beaten you to it, you put yours after theirs, and so on down the line. The exception was the top of the bill. If they had a number in their act the same as yours you took yours out. It was an unwritten law that they always had the first choice of songs. Our turn came to take a run through of our music. I handed the band parts to the trumpets, violins, piano player and the conductor. When I heard laughter coming from the trumpet section I looked down into the orchestra at the lead trumpet.

'Everything all right?' I asked.

He looked up, grinning. 'When was the last time you looked at your band parts?

I shrugged my shoulders.

He pointed to my sheet of music and said: 'It says, "This act gets worse by Thursday."'

The whole orchestra roared with laughter as the trumpet player stood up and handed me my sheet of music. This message, written in longhand, would no doubt have provided great amusement in theatre after theatre.

I handed the sheet music back saying: 'Sorry about that.'

'No problem,' he said. 'I'll let you know on Friday.'

More laughter from the orchestra.

I'm pleased to say that when Friday night came, we looked down into the orchestra pit at the end of our act and were met with the sight of twelve musicians playing our exit music while the conductor gave us a huge thumbs-up sign.

Both of us were working as 1949 came to a close. We did a couple of revues, *Radio Revels* was one, and the other was a talent show called *Personality Parade*. That's where I did my *X-Factor* bit.

In the first half of the show we had a variety bill. There were all sorts of different types of acts: a comic, a boy-and-girl dancing act, an accordionist, an adagio act, and many others. The second half was a band on stage, with me fronting and conducting it, or rather kidding the public I was conducting. I waggled my hands a lot, jumped about a bit and smiled all the time. The band leader was in the band itself so it didn't matter what I did. They just kept playing and took no notice of me.

I was there to introduce the acts that had come to be discovered, or – in nine cases out of ten – be found out. Whenever we had a little girl singing or an elderly person trying to do acrobatics they were always showstoppers. All the relations would come out of the woodwork to see a member of their family try for fame, just like today. Well, maybe not quite like today. But there's nothing much new in show business, despite all the new technology available if you're a performer: the autocue, bluescreen, special effects. But talent? Well, that's a bit more difficult to come by.

By the end of 1950 Beryl had gone home to look after her mother who had become ill after a seizure. It was while Beryl was there that she found out she was pregnant. Her mother's condition was such that there was no way Beryl could return to the theatre. I returned to doing a single spot. I dragged out the old impressions and got a job in *Ladies First*, a touring revue where I did a comedy act and worked with the comic of the show and Charles Cole. Charles was a cartoonist of some note in those days, and his claim to fame was his contribution to the comic *Film Fun* – Leo the Lion was his long-running strip.

Charles was doing a balloon act and he wanted me to join him on stage. This meant I had to learn how to blow balloons up and then twist them into fantastic shapes. I had seen it done in London's West End by an American, Wally Boag, who described himself as a balloon-designing speciality act. He made the balloons into animals and fantastic shapes at breakneck speed with music to match. Charles's act was slightly slower in tempo, but it worked well. It certainly made my lungs stronger, blowing all those balloons up. They were very, very thin and you had to get a huge breath ready before you let go the air into the balloon. I nearly fainted the first time I did this – the blood rushes to your head, you go dizzy and you can get close to passing out. I made it clear we were to be partners for that one show only.

Charles didn't suffer fools gladly. We were playing the Empire Cinema, Walthamstow, in London, and both of us were on stage when an egg came crashing down from the gallery. I got the fright of my young life but Charles never flinched and just continued talking. Then another egg landed on the stage, this time a little nearer to Charles than the last one. Their aim is getting better, I thought. The third one was spot on and landed flush on Charles's head. He stopped. Wiping his face with his hand, and looking up in the direction from where the egg had come, Charles said in the politest of tones: 'Sir [he took it for granted that no lady would do such a thing], twenty years ago I played this theatre and, who knows, you may be throwing eggs at your own father.'

With that remark greeted by stony silence, he continued with the act. It was the politest way I have ever heard anyone called a bastard.

14

The Blue Lamp

I decided to try my luck in London after the *Ladies First* tour came to an end. I wanted to return to doing some filming – if I could – for a change. A casting director asked if I would like to try for a mini-part in the new Alexander Korda film being made at Shepperton Studios. It was *Anna Karenina* and the stars were going to be Vivien Leigh, Ralph Richardson and Kieron Moore.

I arrived at the studios and it was like entering a country mansion. I was ushered into a big room and sitting behind a huge desk was Julien Duvivier, the famous French director. He had a couple of people standing behind him and I was offered a seat in front of the great man. One of the men behind Duvivier leaned forward and said something in French to him. They both looked at me and then Duvivier turned to the other man and said something, again in French. The third man then came into the conversation – in French, of course. Up to this moment no one had said a word in English to me. I sat there wondering what all this was about.

Suddenly, the first man spoke – in English this time.

'Thank you for coming. You have the part. See the young lady at the desk on the way out.'

I did so and she told me I was to play a guest in the big ballroom scene of the film. I had no name. I was just to be one of five guests who would be in this scene dancing and talking. She could tell me no more than that. No matter – it was work.

The day of the shoot arrived and I was kitted out in white tie and tails and covered in facial hair: impressive sideboards and a moustache. No expense had been spared on the set – it was wonderful, a ballroom to end all ballrooms.

My first glimpse of one of our film's stars was Vivien Leigh coming onto the set. Duvivier rushed up to her and covered her with kisses. She smiled at him and spoke in French. He listened, and then replied, again, in French. And that was how the day progressed. Every time the shooting stopped he would talk to her in French and she would reply in kind. All this time her leading man, Kieron Moore would be standing like a lemon not being included in the conversation at all. I watched as close-ups were taken of Leigh and Moore. Every time the scene ended they parted company and most times the director and the leading lady ended up talking away in French. There was a very strained atmosphere during the four days I was there filming. I never got to utter a word. I was a glorified extra, I suppose.

It was about this time that my father took a hand in my career. He knew I was trying to get into films so he rang J. Arthur Rank and, much to my amazement, got me an appointment with a casting director. The meeting ultimately came to nothing but I was still astonished he managed to get me the interview at all. It takes some nerve to pick up the phone and get through to speak to the biggest name in films at that time. I don't know how he did it. Dad would have made a great theatrical agent had he thought about using his talent in that direction . . .

Never one to give up, his other attempt at helping my film career involved him applying for the position of butler to Sir Laurence Olivier. He was invited down to Notley Abbey, about halfway between London and Stratford-upon-Avon, the home Sir Laurence always said was his greatest joy.

His interview didn't last long. Sir Laurence wanted Dad to be able to drive too, as he would be coming down from London late at night by train and Dad would be expected to pick him up by car and drive him back to Notley Abbey. In short, it would seem Sir Laurence needed a butler who could attend to his many guests' needs: serve at table, rise early to light fires, act as chauffeur, head cook, and bottle washer.

After listening to all the duties he would be required to carry out at Notley, Dad then let it be known to Sir Laurence (unwisely I think) that he had a son who was making his way in the theatre and films. When asked what that had to do with him being employed as his butler, Dad said if he accepted the position offered would there be a chance that Sir Laurence could help his son's advancement in the theatrical profession? This was a question that Sir Laurence evidently thought should never have been asked, and he said so quite forcibly.

At this point Dad decided that the interview was at an end and in his own inimitable way, told Sir Laurence where to place the post that had been offered to him. It would seem he left Notley Abbey rather more quickly than he arrived.

When Dad told me this story my only reaction was to tersely say: 'Stick to phoning.'

Anyway, I gave him full marks for trying. But I also hoped that Sir Laurence wouldn't remember the Buckland name and get me blackballed from the whole acting profession. I needn't have worried really – by this time, I had changed my name. It had happened quite by accident. I was visiting Beryl, who was doing one of her William Henshall revues. Willie was quite a character and he and his wife Evelyn had become very friendly with Beryl. I was talking to Willie one night by the side of the stage when, suddenly, out of nowhere, he said, 'Buckland's too long.'

I was taken aback. I asked him what on earth he meant.

'It's not good for your billing,' he replied. 'It takes up too much space on a bill.'

I started to get interested. After all, this was advice from a big producer who had been putting on shows for years.

'You mean change my name?' I said, with some degree of doubt in my voice. I questioned him as to what he thought would be the right sort of name.

'Something short and snappy,' he replied.

'OK, give me a name,' I shot back at him.

He came back with 'Michaels'. But at the time, I'd never heard the name Michaels (which is of Jewish origin). In fact, I thought he'd said Michael. I turned the name over and over in my head, repeating it out loud several times, *Glenn Michael, Glenn Michael.* I decided from that moment on that I was to be known as Glenn Michael (note the double 'n'). A variety bill was printed for one of the dates I was playing with one 'n' dropped one from Glenn, leaving Glen Michael. That name – and that spelling – stuck.

I had been thinking of a name change for some time. Wee Jock Kerr from my Gang Show days had said Coe would be a good name for me. I think he was taking the mickey – imagine working in Scotland with a name like Glen Coe . . . Mind you, as Willie Henshall might have said, it would have looked big on a bill!

It was about this time that I had a lucky break. I had been mooching about, doing bits and pieces in a few films that are best forgotten, when I got a call to audition for a film being made at Ealing Studios. Sir Michael Balcon had recently made a big impact at the studios, bringing in talented editors and writers like Alexander Mackendrick and Basil Dearden and giving them jobs directing. Sir Michael was also actively seeking new screenwriters whom he thought deserved a chance. In the process he discovered T.E.B. Clarke, who won an Oscar for scripting *The Lavender Hill Mob* and who also wrote the famous *Passport to Pimlico*. Clarke was then asked to script the first documentary-style police drama. It was eventually called *The Blue Lamp*. (I still have the original shooting script and it's over an inch thick!)

I was asked to go along to Ealing Studios and meet the director of this new film, Basil Dearden, and producer Michael Relph. Basil Dearden was sitting in a small armchair, hunched up, his face in his hands. Michael Relph, was sitting very formally at a desk and I sat in front of him. We shook hands and he started to tell me the story of the film.

It would be about the everyday life of a policeman. Jack Warner was to star – he was an experienced variety performer from radio shows like *Garrison Theatre*, and was now establishing himself as a serious actor. The male lead was to be a new young actor called Dirk Bogarde. Dirk had just come out of the army as a young officer and they thought he had star potential. Peggy Evans was the love interest.

'I think you would be ideal for the barrow-boy part,' said Michael Relph. 'It's not a huge part but you can make it into something on the set. What have you done before?'

I started to tell him of my bit-parts in films and of my work in variety. All this time Basil Dearden had been as still as stone in his chair. He hadn't moved an inch, and had never taken his eyes off me for a second. I was beginning to feel somewhat uncomfortable. I was still talking when he interrupted my flow.

'Larry Davis,' he said, moving in his chair for the first time.

'Sorry?' said Michael Relph, turning in his chair to look in astonishment at Dearden. 'Larry Davis?'

Basil Dearden grinned as he said: 'Ideal, bright, young. Yes . . . perfect Larry.'

He looked over at me and gave a great big grin. I just sat, my heart thumping, wondering what was going to come next.

Michael Relph, visibly perturbed, argued, 'But Basil, we've already given that part to Glyn Houston [brother of film star Donald Houston].'

'Doesn't matter,' said Mr Dearden. 'He can do the barrow-boy part.'

Basil Dearden pushed himself out of his chair and took me outside to where a young lady was sitting. He introduced me to a young actress, Jennifer Jayne (who sadly died in 2006 after doing many film and stage roles in her career). Basil explained that she was to be my girlfriend in the film. We were to play an argumentative young couple that comes out of a cinema to witness Jack Warner (as the policeman) get shot by Dirk Bogarde. There would also be other scenes with Bernard Lee set in the police station. Bernard later became best known as M in the James Bond films, and was a very fine actor. But what a sense of humour he had.

When I was filming a scene at the police station, we had to do a lot of cutaway shots and over-the-shoulder shots where you only saw Bernard's back on the edge of the frame and a close-up of Jennifer and my face over his shoulder looking directly at the camera. Bernard had no lines in these shots. He just stood there facing us while we did our bit to camera. But despite Bernard having nothing to say, his face was working overtime. At rehearsals everything was fine, but as soon as the cameras started to roll, Bernard started to roll – his eyes, his nose, his lips . . . You name it, Bernard did it. Of course Jennifer and I both forgot our lines and started to giggle. We would get into trouble from Basil Dearden, while Bernard got away with murder.

Jack Warner was a gem of a guy. Breaks in his filming would often lead to Jack joining me when I was watching a scene and we'd chat. Despite our age difference I think he thought we had something in common having both played in variety. He always said how lucky he was to be able to work in a film like *The Blue Lamp* when he knew things would be winding down for him in light entertainment.

I remember doing a Sunday concert with him in Wales during shooting. We shared a dressing room and as I was getting ready for the show, hanging my suit up and laying my make-up out, I noticed Jack was looking down at the dressing table in front of him. He was seated in front of the mirror and looked depressed.

'What's up?' I asked. Too bluntly, perhaps.

'I'm lost,' he said. I really thought he was ill.

'Can I help?' I offered, not knowing what else to say.

'I've forgotten how to do my stage make-up, Glen,' he admitted ruefully. 'They always do our make-up when we're filming . . . Makes us lazy. You'll have to remind me. What numbers do I use, for God's sake?'

We both laughed at the situation and I was delighted to think the great Jack Warner, star of stage and screen, had to ask me for advice. It just so happened I was using pancake stage make-up which comes in a round, flat, tin with, in my case, a tan shade inside it. You dampened a sponge, squeezed it thoroughly, and then swept it over the make-up to apply to your face. Result? It turned a pale, white, ill-looking face into a tanned, healthy-looking Hollywood god. Of course, it couldn't alter the shape, but that's another story. Jack had dug up some old cigar-shaped make-up sticks and he wanted to know how he could get a tanned effect with them. I offered him the use of my make-up but he refused as he wanted to do his own. I explained that a 5 and a 9 would give him a tan. He laughed and said now it was all coming back to him; he put the white 5 on his face then mixed in the stick of yellow 9. The end result looked as if he'd been under a sun lamp for a fortnight.

In the course of making *The Blue Lamp* I also had the chance to have a few chats with Dirk Bogarde, whom I found to be very pleasant indeed. He would sometimes seek me out at a tea break and we would talk about my days in the RAF and his in the army. I did feel a little in awe of him, because he was the star of the film and I was a very minor player.

Assistant director Harry Kratz took me aside one day and asked what Mr Bogarde had been talking to me about. I told him and asked why he wanted to know.

'No reason,' he replied and I left it at that.

After a few days Harry came to me again.

'Why does Dirk talk to you so much?' he asked again.

I got a little angry and said I couldn't stop the star talking to me if he wanted to.

'Well, don't get involved Glen. I mean it,' And with that, he returned to the set. I never had a conversation Mr Bogarde again, except when filming Jack Warner being shot in the cinema foyer, which was filmed at the Metropole Theatre, not far from the Edgware Road.

That brought back memories of when Beryl and I did our double act at the old Met when the top of the bill was G.H. Elliot, known as 'The Original Chocolate-coloured Coon'. He was a giant of the old-time music halls and this was his farewell tour, though I understand he did about twenty subsequent farewell tours after that one!

Elliot would sing one of his own compositions 'I Used to Sigh for the Silvery Moon,' and when he'd got the audience singing along he'd leave the stage to change his costume. I was backstage watching him do it one night and it was fascinating to see; he was so calm. He came off stage to where his second wife June had his next outfit ready, laid out on a large, spotless, white sheet. He sat on a chair and carefully changed his shoes, socks, trousers, shirt, before finally donning his Panama hat. This would all take three minutes or more, and while he was doing this, the audience would still be singing along with the orchestra. Eventually he would dance back on stage to cheers and continue the performance. How many performers today could do that, I wonder? You always learn something if you watch performers back-stage. That night I was taught how to control an audience. Elliot was a master.

In *The Blue Lamp* the shots of the bar in the Old Metropole, where you could have a drink while watching through the long glass wall that separated the bar from the auditorium, were just as I remember when we played there with our double act, Michael and Raye.

Most of the night-time filming for *The Blue Lamp* was done in the Harrow Road. The stunt drivers were nice guys who worked very hard at making everything look as real as possible.

One scene required a car to come tearing down the road at breakneck speed chased by a police car. We had roadworks set up and the stuntmen had to drive at the barriers, crash through them, and carry on down the road as fast as they could. They rehearsed it again and again without using the barriers.

It got to about four o'clock in the morning and director Basil Dearden decided they would go for a 'take'. He instructed the stunt driver of the first car to go down to the end of the road and be ready for his signal to start – a wave of the director's handkerchief. The stuntman got in the car and drove down to the end of the road. It was a fair distance. We watched him turn the car and park it facing the camera. He was ready for the signal to start his spectacular crash run.

Meanwhile, it was discovered many of the barriers were not in the right place. So they had to get out the drawings and check that they were in the correct position and that the camera angles were set correctly.

After a lot of to-ing and fro-ing, out came the hankie and Dearden signalled the driver to set off. He called 'Action!' You could have heard a pin drop on that fine, but cold, night in old London town. After a long pause we all realised that the car wasn't moving. There was more frantic waving. The car still didn't move. Our assistant director, who was carrying a bit of weight I might add, was told to run down to the car and see what was happening. After what seemed like ages he returned, out of breath and panting like a St Bernard. Dearden asked what the problem was.

'He'd fallen asleep,' gasped Harry, on the verge of collapsing himself. Our stunt man had been waiting so long for the signal he'd literally 'crashed-out' and had been in a deep sleep.

Once roused, our driver made no mistake. The stunt was a spectacular 'first take' success as the car smashed through the barriers perfectly. Directors are always thrilled if you can do anything on the first take because rehearsing and rehearsing eventually erodes the natural quality of the performance. Spencer Tracy always said, 'If it don't work on the first take it'll never work.' I've always remembered that. In my TV days I was always known as 'first-take Michael'.

The Blue Lamp was finally finished and the premiere was arranged for the Empire, Leicester Square. It was a big night but Beryl couldn't attend because she was in pantomime as Cinderella at the Guildhall, Southampton. I still decided that I would splash out and arranged for Harrods of Knightsbridge to send a Rolls Royce to pick up my father and mother, and then pick me up so that we would arrive in appropriate style.

We would all go in evening dress. Mum looked lovely, as always. Dad? Well, he looked like Dad: hair brushed back in his usual style and in a dinner suit that had seen a hundred stately dining rooms up and down the British Isles. I wore what I thought was the latest in American-style big-shouldered dinner suits. We all set off feeling like stars.

When we got to the square it was packed with people and we had some trouble getting to the front of the theatre. In front of us in the line of traffic was a filthy looking MG Sports car that insisted on holding us up by crawling along. I really didn't know what on earth it could be doing there. I instructed the chauffeur to sound his horn and he did so with absolutely no reaction from the other driver. As the line of cars pulled up and one by one the occupants left their vehicles to walk up the red carpet, the MG stayed in front of us. To my astonishment it too pulled up at the red carpet. I shouted at our chauffeur to hoot his horn once again and he did so – again to no avail. The doors of the MG opened and from the passenger side out stepped the elegantly dressed and beautiful Jean Simmons. On the driver's side was Dirk Bogarde. A young man jumped into the car and drove it off to park it . . .

We pulled up in our Rolls and our chauffeur ran round to open our door. Mum and Dad stepped out onto the red carpet, closely followed by me. I was smiling and waving in reaction to the cheers and applause – it was a wonderful reception for anyone walking the red carpet that night.

I turned around just in time to see my dear father put his hand in his pocket and in the loudest of voices say to the chauffeur: 'What do we owe you?'

There was a titter of laughter from some of the crowd who were near enough to hear this and I was absolutely mortified. I'd wanted everyone to think the Rolls was mine (as if!) and grabbed my father before he could improve on his latest gaff by offering the chauffeur a tip or even inviting him to join us. Waving and smiling, we walked the carpet and entered the cinema to take our seats in the circle.

At the end of the film we stood amidst tumultuous cheering and clapping. Dad turned to me and said: 'Where's the newsreel?' Above the continuing noise I pointed out that this was a premiere showing and not a 1s 9d flick at the local picture house. He seemed very disappointed.

Everyone was raving about the film and after some time I managed to get a taxi for my parents, and they left me to enjoy the after-show party. Many people think that if you're in show business, socialising and mixing with people should be second nature to you. This is simply not so. Many big stars are naturally very shy people. I remember asking Rikki Fulton at my son's wedding if he'd like to say a few words and he was petrified. He preferred to sit quietly in a corner, enjoying himself in his own way, with his wife, Kate.

I'm very like that as well and can be quite shy at social occasions. It was just so at *The Blue Lamp* party. But I managed to put on a brave face most of the time and when Basil Dearden came over to talk to me I was very at ease with him. As the director it was flattering that he sought me out amongst so many stars. The conversation that followed amid the chatter and noise was most enlightening.

Basil's opening remark shook me a little: 'You have a problem. You look too much like Dirk Bogarde on camera. Did you know that?'

I had to admit I didn't.

'Problem number two is that you have no agent. You must get yourself a good agent.'

Before I could answer he carried on.

'I've talked to a pal of mine, John Glidden; he'll see you next week. He's in Mayfair . . . The address is in the book.'

At that he turned to greet a woman who was bearing down on us. 'Darling, how good of you to come.' Taking her arm, he led her away.

The wind had been taken right out of my sails and if I'd been a boat I'd have capsized, gone down with all hands. I was so shocked at what Basil had said that I left the party soon after.

When I got back to our flat, I looked for John Glidden's address in the telephone directory. Sure enough he was in Mayfair. I rang him first thing the next morning and was told by a very pleasant-sounding lady that Mr Glidden would be delighted to see me at 3 p.m. that very day. I couldn't wait for the clock hands to reach the magic hour.

On arrival at the imposing frontage of this Mayfair address, the lady who had first answered my call walked me down a long oak-lined corridor and opened a door. A very large room was revealed and on the wall facing me was a huge painting of a lady in a theatrical costume. As I walked towards the gigantic desk in front of it and approached the man sitting behind it, the face of the beautiful lady in the painting became clear to me. It was Vivien Leigh.

'Lovely, isn't she?' said Mr Glidden. 'Everyone does that – sees her first, then me.'

He invited me to sit down and told me that he was indeed Vivien Leigh's manager along with Michael Rennie and a few other very well-known actors and actresses. I studied this impressive-looking man with his iron-grey hair and a face that wouldn't have gone amiss on a big screen.

'Basil Dearden says you could be another Ian Carmichael; would you like to be?'

I nodded, smiled and shrugged my shoulders.

'I'll take that as a yes,' he smiled back at me and then started to write in the book in front of him. 'We'll have a go at the Crown Film Unit for starters,' he said.

I knew they were the government film unit that produced and shot advertisements on health, food, and other public issues. Not exactly the stuff of Hollywood, I thought.

He told me that I could only expect to start in a small way as regarded fees.

'We'll start low . . . Just to tease 'em. How about £200?'

'A week?' I nearly screamed out in joy.

'A day, old son, a day,' he whispered with a smile.

I duly signed a contract and left the office – not just on cloud nine, but approaching what could have been cloud ten. I though I was on my way to Hollywood.

My dreams started to fade when I was called by Mr Glidden's office a few days later. He told me he was waiting for a phone call from the Crown Film Unit. The phone rang while I was there and a conversation ensued where he said no a few times, yes a few times, then, 'A hundred and seventy-five, no can do, bye.'

He told me they'd offered me £175 a day for a four-day shoot and he'd turned it down. I begged him to ring them back and take it. I could see £700 floating in front of my eyes – a fortune to me. He refused to do this saying they'd ring back. I left feeling very down.

There was no further word from Mr Glidden. Then I got a letter saying he was retiring but the office would continue to represent me. I got offers through his office for all sorts of different things that paid no money but they said would be good for my image.

But image alone doesn't pay the bills. I began to think I would have to go back to working on the stage to earn some cash.

15

A family man

The year 1951 came in with a bang. On 31 March, Beryl gave birth to a baby girl in St Mary's Village Hospital, Prestbury, in the county of Cheshire. Beryl loved this little village and we had decided that Prestbury would look much better on our baby's birth certificate than Bacup, industrial Lancashire, where she had been staying with her parents. I suppose you can put this decision down to us being young twits. As a result, Yonnie, our lovely little girl, was nearly born en route to hospital in the ambulance as Prestbury was much further away than the nearest maternity hospital.

Sadly, I was away working when this happened and I missed all the fun. I was touring in another edition of *Ladies First*. Once again I was doing comedy and enjoying it. While I was on tour I had an offer to do a summer season at the Priory Theatre, Whitley Bay, near Newcastle. We arranged digs for the three of us: Beryl and I, and our new arrival, three-month-old Yonnie. It was a very nice boarding house, not very far from the theatre on the shore.

I would have to find different acts to do in five changes of programme. I had never had to do this before so I had to get the old brain box cracking and find some new material. We started on 16 June and our last week was to be 27 August, a 'request week' programme. In between we had; 'Sidewalks of New York', 'Memories of Jolson', 'Cowboy Capers', 'Fifty Happy Years' and 'A Wee Bit of Scotch'.

Eddie Morrell presented the show. He was a Morecambe-based comedian who also ran a summer season in Morecambe on the Central Pier. Our show had a cast of thirteen and consisted of comic Harry Neil, who was well known in the north of England; Al Shaw, a famous radio name, with his electric guitar; Ena and Elma Gerard, a Scottish act; a couple of singers; and four charming young lady dancers who worked their socks off.

Oh, and I nearly forgot. We also had a young man at the piano who played during the entire show. When he performed it was as if an entire orchestra was playing and he went on to become a very well-known composer. His name was Peter Greenwell.

The show was called *Starlights* and our opening chorus went something like this:

The Starlights are shining tonight,
The Starlights so happy and bright,
There may be a moon over London way,
But the Starlights are shining on Whitley Bay.

All thirteen of us would dance up and down a tiny stage in boiling hot weather. We were dressed in full white tie and tails for the men and evening gowns for the ladies. I still have a colour programme that has 3d on the cover and the bill matter for the show says, 'No. 7 spot: Glen Michael, "Spinning a Yarn".' (I'll bet the act was hand-knitted too!)

Our dressing rooms at the back of the theatre looked onto the permanent fairground where music was played all day long. The trouble was, they played the same songs over and over again. All summer I had to endure Frankie Laine singing 'Mule Train' – complete with sound effects of cracking whips. I played it on Saga FM more recently on my Saturday-night *Show Stoppers* programme and still cringed. The other thing that stands out from that season of fun and laughter was when Beryl and I were in the early hours of the morning by the sound of bagpipes and singing. It was a frightening sound to wake up to. When the landlady told us it was the beginning of Scots Week she laughed and said we'd get used to it.

We did. What a time the Scots contingent had on holiday. When they came into the theatre they really enjoyed themselves and the show. It was my first encounter with a Scottish audience. I liked them enormously and they seemed to like me as a performer.

The summer season at Whitley Bay was a big success. Much to my delight, on the last week of our season I received a letter offering me the summer season at Morecambe to take part in the sister *Starlights* show for Eddie Morrell. I accepted knowing I wouldn't have to learn a new opening chorus. It just meant singing that the *Starlights* were shining on Morecambe instead of Whitley Bay – how lazy can you get? It was going to be a long summer season at Morecambe so Beryl and I decided to look for a flat. We found one right on the shorefront, one floor up and with sea views. We moved in a few weeks before rehearsals started.

Yonnie used to sit in her high chair near the window when the window cleaner came. He was a very nice young man who would always clean the kitchen window first, making faces all the while at Yonnie, who loved his antics. One day, he began his cleaning and made faces to keep Yonnie laughing as usual. She started to wave at him and play peek-a-boo. Yonnie waved, he waved back, she made a funny face, he made one back at her, she bobbed down in her chair, the window cleaner bobbed down . . . But didn't come back up again at the window. There was no sign of him. Beryl screamed, I shouted, and Yonnie continued to think all of this was a great game and kept playing peek-a-boo at the empty window. I found our window cleaner lying on the concrete floor having just fallen from our first-floor window.

Amazingly, he was unhurt, and he started laughing as he tried to stagger to his feet. 'No harm done,' he said as he dusted himself off. I made him stay still and it was only afterwards we realised that the shoes he'd had on had helped save him from serious injury. (I later called them 'Francie and Josie' shoes as they had thick crepe soles in a Teddy Boy style)

One day in Morecambe I spotted a car I liked in a garage – a huge Daimler with a throttle on the steering wheel. I bought it for £75 and when I drove it away I was as proud as punch. When I think back now I must have been daft to even look at it. I used to drive along the prom at Morecambe on my way to rehearsals on the Central Pier with my feet sticking out of the passenger front window while I used the throttle on the steering wheel as the accelerator. I would always get smiles and waves from holidaymakers. If you tried that nowadays you would be charged with something, but it was fun in the days when there were fewer cars on the road.

One day there was a lull in rehearsals and I decided I would improve the look of my new car by painting it. None of your respray jobs for me – I would do it myself. I liked the colour but I thought I would brighten it up a bit. I bought some tins of varnish and one sunny and hot day I varnished the entire car. I started doing this in the garage at about 9 a.m. and was finished by 4 p.m.

By doing it myself I reckoned I'd saved loads of cash. I was so pleased that, after a quick shower, I decided to show the world my creation. I got in the car and set off along Morecambe promenade. It was around 5 p.m. and I could see I was getting lots of smiles, people were waving and laughing and I waved and smiled back. I pulled up at the pier. When I got out I instantly realised why I'd been attracting so much attention. I put my finger onto the wing of my car and it was still sticky. And the entire car appeared to be covered in every insect known to man. Midges, bees, flies, as well as dust and fluff – it was all there in abundance. I had a massive motorcar flypaper. People began asking me if this was an advert for the show or a stunt and even called me Fly-man; the suggestions came thick and fast. I drove back to our flat wondering what I was going to tell Beryl. Happily, she just laughed. I'm still the very worst DIY man ever.

The *Starlights* turned out to be a very happy season in Morecambe. Eddie Morrell was a favourite in the town and he was the ideal Lancashire comic for a coastal summer show. The acts were good and we played to full houses. The matinees were another story, though. They relied so much on the weather. The show would be cancelled on sunny days because nobody wanted to sit indoors. Eddie would ring everyone at lunchtime to tell us whether we had to perform or not.

He got it wrong one dreary Monday morning. The grey clouds were rolling over the sea towards Morecambe and heading for the Central Pier. I had a feeling the phone would ring around lunchtime and Eddie Morrell would be telling me I'd be performing that afternoon. Sure enough the phone rang and we had a 2 p.m. show to do. The cast were all made up and ready when, at 1.50 p.m., the sun suddenly broke through the clouds and began blazing down. Eddie put his head around the door of my dressing room (I had moved up in the world and had a room to myself).

'It doesn't look good,' he said. 'Just do the best you can.'

I slipped on my tail jacket and made for the stage. There were only 70 people in a theatre that could hold 500. Talk about peas in a drum.

But among the small crowd were the legendary comic actress Thora Hird (a friend of Eddie's as they both came from Morecambe) and her young daughter Janette Scott. In fact, they were sitting in the front row.

I pulled out all the stops my comedy spot and it was probably one of my best shows. Small though the audience was, they made our company feel they had enjoyed the efforts of the Starlights on a very hot and sunny day.

As I was washing off my make-up, a knock at the door made me grab a towel and drape it over my shoulders. I was half expecting Eddie to bring Thora Hird and her daughter in to be introduced. When I opened the door there was a sight that could have come straight out of *Harry Potter*. I was faced by a lady of average height, dressed all in black, with a black cloak a small black hat, black horn-rimmed glasses and a whitish face. For a moment she looked me up and down, then she clicked her teeth together (which were obviously false) in preparation for finally speaking to me. I'd seen comics do this on stage to get a laugh and I had to stifle one myself. She waved a small umbrella at me.

'Hello, my name's Nellie Sutherland,' she clattered in a voice which had a distinct Scottish inflection to it. 'I've just been in to see the show and you were very good.'

I thought she wanted my autograph and my first reaction was to reach for my pen. As I turned to look for it she carried on talking and stepped into my dressing room, shutting the door behind her as she continued talking.

'Have you ever worked in Scotland?'

All I could think of was how to get this lady out of my dressing room.

Without taking a breath she continued, teeth clattering away. 'I represent W.R. Gault of Glasgow. We're a theatrical agency and I'm looking for someone like you to work with an up-and-coming young comic in Scotland. We like to use English performers for what I have in mind. You could do your own comedy spots and also be a feed for the comic. The money's not big but it would be regular work.'

I was taken completely aback and, to be honest, I didn't believe her. I thought she was slightly deranged and had wandered backstage and simply picked on me (believe me, it does happen!)

I played for time.

'That's very interesting,' I said. It was all I could think of.

'I'll write to you,' she clattered as she moved towards the door. 'It would mean you starting in November. Are you booked for later in the year?'

'No, no,' I laughed nervously as I guided her towards and out of my dressing room door.

'I'll be in touch,' she said. With a wave of her umbrella and a final clatter of teeth, she was gone.

Later, Eddie did bring Thora and Janette round to see the company and we found them both charming. Thora had enjoyed the show and Janette smiled sweetly. It's strange to think now that Janette would one day marry singing legend Mel Tormé and Thora would eventually become a dame and a much-loved star of many films and TV comedy series.

I soon forgot all about my visitor in black, but about a week later I received a letter from W.R. Gault, Theatrical Agency, Sauchiehall Street, Glasgow. It contained a formal offer of five weeks' work at the Victory Theatre, Paisley as feed to the comic and to work 'as required' in the show on the understanding I could also do my own comedy spot. If satisfactory to both parties it could become a permanent position. I was offered £20 a week – a good wage in 1952. The name of the comic I was to be teamed up with was Jack Milroy. It was just another name and meant nothing to me.

After signing the contract and sending it back I had second thoughts. I had been told there was talk of me being offered more film work, but it was only a maybe, and I had a wife, not to mention a daughter now, to think about. Regular income made it seem the right thing to do. But I had never set foot over the border before. I had played all the dumps you could mention in England as far up as Carlisle. Beryl had the edge on me there as she had played in Edinburgh and Glasgow in the *Peter Pan* production starring Ann Todd and Alastair Sim. She told me it was a lovely country and she had found the people to be very friendly. I felt a lot better about my decision after that conversation.

The *Starlights* season in Morecambe continued to play to good houses. My comedy spots were going well: so well, in fact, that Eddie Morrell offered me a pantomime. I was to play Granny Hood and Beryl was to be Robbie, the principal boy, in his production of *Red Riding Hood* at the Theatre Royal, Stockport.

Beryl was delighted – the Royal held fond memories for her. Her father had owned it at one time. It had hosted posh productions by Tyrone Guthrie, the famous stage director, with the Old Vic Company from London, one of which had starred a very young John Gielgud as leading man. But that was all in the past. By 1952 it presented mostly small revues and variety shows, and, of course, pantomimes like the one we were going to perform in that winter. It meant I would have to leave Paisley at the end of my five-week stint and rush down to Stockport, going straight into rehearsals to open on Christmas Eve. It would be tight, but we could do it.

The contract with Eddie Morrell Productions said twice-nightly performances at 6.20 p.m. and 8.30 p.m., with matinees daily at 2.30 p.m. That meant a total of twenty-eight shows a week, three shows a day. You arrived at the theatre just after 1 p.m. and you came out – with luck – at the back of 11 p.m. They made 'em tough in our day – you had to be with the 'no play, no pay' threat hanging over you.

The end of the season arrived. It was time for me to go to Scotland.

16

Off to Scotland

On 15 November 1952, I found myself driving over Shap in Cumbria heading for Glasgow. It was a cold winter's day and my old Daimler was straining under its load of two adults, an eighteen-month-old baby, a pram, nappies, and various cases holding all we had in the world. How I hoped Jock Kerr's words would ring true: 'You'll love Scotland.'

At exactly 12 noon, I drew up at the old post office in Paisley and asked the way to the Victory Theatre. In those days the post office in any town was the community's information centre. They knew everything about anything and anyone. I was directed to the theatre and as I drove up I was delighted to see it was a small, cosy-looking place. I popped into the chemist that was opposite the theatre – although perhaps I should say 'al-chemist' as the gentleman who appeared from the back of the shop looked like an extra from Lord of the Rings. He had a bald, dome-like head with long, straggly hair that hung from just above his ears down to cascade over his shoulders. He looked at me with suspicious but kindly eyes. I asked if the theatre would be opening soon and much to my surprise he replied in a very cultured voice. 'No, it's closed in the afternoon and opens around 5 p.m. Or rather, the stage door will be. Are you going to be in the new show?'

'Yes, I am, as a matter of fact. It looks like a nice theatre,' I added, more by way of conversation than anything else.

'I remember when hansom cabs drawn by big black horses used to pull up at the front and out would step ladies and gents in full evening dress,' he said, looking back across at the theatre.

'You remember that?' I asked politely.

'Lord, yes! I was just a wee boy and regularly used to sit in our window watching the comings and goings.'

I left this charming old man with his memories and his huge bottles of potions. We found the Todholm Inn overlooking Paisley, which was up a long hill and is sadly no longer there. The landlord and his wife greeted us with a smile and showed us to our small but neat bedroom.

Winter in Paisley was very cold. After having some tea I thought I would go down to the theatre. Beryl and Yonnie were better off staying in the hotel to try to thaw out. I got to the Victory Theatre to discover there was a show on called *Hot from Harlem*. The stage manager was a nice guy and when I introduced myself he allowed me to stand on the side of the stage and watch the show from the wings.

As I was enjoying this privilege, I was aware of a young lady beside me who was warbling softly as she readied herself to go on stage. I made way for her and she gave a warm smile and thanked me. She sang her heart out and came off to tremendous applause. As she left the stage I turned to the stage manager and remarked what a wonderful performer she was. I asked her name and he said: 'She's only seventeen . . . I think she's called Shirley Bassey.'

The following day I went into the theatre by the front door and took a seat in the back stalls. No one could see me and I found myself watching a group of people on stage obviously rehearsing some sort of sketch. I could not believe what I was hearing. The man standing with his back to me was talking – well, screaming might be a better way of describing it.

'Don't you know what you're f★★★ing doing?'

'What do you want, a f★★★ing nursemaid?'

'You're all a bunch of arseholes!'

'You have to learn these lines, you bastards.'

My heart began thumping and a major panic set in. I dashed out of my seat to the front of house where I found the manager and practically dragged him to the back stalls. Pointing at the stage I gasped: 'Tell me, is that Jack Milroy talking to those unfortunate people?'

He looked at me as if I was mad.

'Good God, no,' said the theatre manager. 'That's Johnny – Johnny Victory. He's always like that.' He walked away laughing.

The relief I felt was palpable and I nearly cried. If that had turned out to be Jack Milroy I'd have been back over Shap that very night with my family.

All the same, when I did eventually meet Jack, my introduction to working with him *was* a little strained. I knew he had been at the Tivoli Theatre, Aberdeen, working with his wife Mary and another feed, Artie Mayn. Working as a feed with a comedian is rather like being married. The feed is the 'caring wife' and the comic has to feel he can rely on the feed no matter what. The comic has to feel comfortable with the feed and although the comic wants his feed to be the best he can be, he also has to be sure he doesn't override the comic and get laughs where the comic doesn't want laughs. A good feed should be able to read moods, speak only when spoken to and be the butt of any joke.

That's the job of a *straight* feed. But I was a *comedy* feed. That means you have to be funny – but only when called upon – and make sure you don't step on the comic's toes in the process. You have to be able to play old men, young men, complete idiots, be an all-round actor but hold it back a bit from being very good or you could be out of a job. If you can do all these things and more, you *might* make a feed.

I had always worked with comics who had been around a long time in show business. They had a set routine and they, or you, didn't move away from that. Jack was different.

In our first show together both Jack and I were a little nervous of each other on stage. We were like a couple of boxers trying to find out each other's strengths and weaknesses. It didn't take me long to see this man was going to be a talented comedian. He had the charm of a young Cary Grant and the drive of a Danny Kaye.

Nothing spectacular happened in those few weeks at the Victory Theatre, Paisley. In fact, I think I upset things a little when I told them I couldn't continue after Paisley as Beryl and I had a pantomime to do in Stockport. At the same time, I was delighted to have been asked to join Jack after our panto finished and was sent a contract that said we would open on 26 January 1953 at the Palace Theatre, Dundee. I was thrilled.

Beryl walked through her part as Robbie in the panto and then calmly told me: 'This might be the end.'

'End of what?' I wanted to know, fearing the worst . . . But it turned out she had been thinking for some time of leaving the business to look after our baby daughter full-time. Beryl felt that working in the theatre simply wasn't compatible with motherhood. It wasn't an easy decision for someone who had been so successful and who loved performing so much.

When I arrived at the theatre in Dundee to begin rehearsals I sensed something wasn't quite right. It worried me. Glen Daly, a fine Scottish artist and singer, had been working with Jack in my place while I had been appearing in panto. As I slipped into my different parts in the show I could tell Jack wasn't happy with my work. He never said anything, but I think that he'd simply got used to Glen Daly working with him and found my style a little strange. Not long after, however, Glen received an offer to join the *Lex McLean Show* in Glasgow and he left. Relations improved between Jack and myself and soon I was the only one who could work with him. I realised that to try to break away and develop a single comedy spot on my own would mean a lot of work on top of learning other sketches, songs and dance routines. So I made a conscious decision to concentrate on working with Jack, building up my parts into larger character roles. We started to do a couple of sketches that looked like they could evolve into something more than just a few seasonal laughs.

One was called 'A Scot in London'. Over the thirteen years we worked together I think it was my favourite sketch. We performed it all over the Scottish theatre circuit from Aberdeen to Glasgow and everywhere in between.

It was a simple story. Jack played a Scot, and was dressed in a flat tartan cap, kilt, sporran and a fine, V-neck jumper. He wore his trademark tackety army boots with tap-shoe plates attached to the sole. His only prop was a small bunch of lucky white heather that he held in his hand. The backcloth was of Piccadilly Circus, setting the scene for my entrance as the typical London spiv. I wore a very broad-shouldered black overcoat tied tightly at the waist a matching black belt, highly polished black shoes, a small trilby hat pulled down over my eyes, and I sported a pencil-thin moustache with long black sideboards. A cheeky London accent completed the character.

Jack would open the scene with his cry of: 'Lucky white heather! Lucky white heather! Get your lucky white heather here!'

That was my cue to walk down from as far upstage as possible. The idea was that Jack didn't see me for quite some time. The audience sensed what was coming and started to laugh as soon as they spotted me. The laughs grew and grew as I very, very slowly made my way down to Jack. He was still crying out 'Lucky white heather' as I reached him. I thoroughly enjoyed the length of time we both took to size each other up. Sometimes we stood looking at each other for ages – me with a sickly smile on my face, a smile of anticipation, and Jack grinning from ear to ear, thinking he had at last got a sale for his heather.

We would get into conversation about money. I'd call it 'masuma' and 'lolly' getting Jack very confused and eventually persuading him to give me some 'lolly' to put on a 'nag' or an 'orse'. In between all this patter the English and Scottish question would be raised – much to the delight of the patriotic Scots audience.

'That's the trouble with all you Scots,' I'd say. 'You're all kill. Look at the names of some of your towns. You've got Kill-syth, Kill-marnock, and another one . . . Kill-Malcolm.'

That would get roars of laughter, and Jack would enlighten me with: 'It's Kilma*colm,* ya mug, ya. And what about you English? With your Tynemouth, Portsmouth and Weymouth. You're all mouth – the lot of you!'

We would both stand there, waiting to continue as the entire theatre erupted with applause, laughter and whistles.

We did this sketch at the Pavilion Theatre in Glasgow and one day, just as I appeared on stage, I was greeted by complete silence and a voice from the gallery as clear as a bell saying: 'Give him the bloody message!' The line was delivered better than any comic could have managed and the timing was perfect. It got roars of laughter, not only from the audience but also from Jack and I, who were curled up on stage with laughter ourselves. That's something you should never do as a professional, but the wonderful Glasgow humour completely got the better of us.

As 1954 progressed, Jack and I took up the offer of a summer season at the Gaiety Theatre in Ayr. It was very well known to English pros because of its reputation as a nursery for talent. And that season would be extra special – it was the twenty-fifth edition of the world-famous *Gaiety Whirl.*

We fixed digs in Ayr with a woman called Aggie and her husband Matt, the drummer in the band at the Gaiety. Aggie was such a character that she could have been a comedian herself. She was, in fact, a cleaner at the theatre. Matt was a first-class theatre drummer – a rare commodity today. He was also an effects man – a vital partner for a comic. I used to do a few comedy stunt falls with Jack. In one sketch I would lean on a walking stick and when Jack felt the need for a big laugh he would kick the stick away and I'd fall down flat onto the stage with a clatter. Matt in the orchestra pit would hit everything in sight on his drum kit at the exact moment I landed on the boards. The result was double the laughter.

The show had a great working cast. There was the Maple Leaf Four – a vocal harmony group from the radio show *Smoky Mountain Jamboree* – who, besides being a great stage act, were full of fun. During the season we did a Scottish programme and it involved a pipe band of around twenty

164

guys who were mostly built like rugby players. As they finished their spot on stage they had to leave playing at full blast. Not knowing the layout of the theatre too well – it was the first performance on the Monday night – they were coming off a dimly lit stage to a pitch-black passage. As the pipe major marched off the Maple Leaf Four were waiting for him. One of them opened the door of a replica phone booth that was on the side of the stage and directly in the pipe major's path.

'This way son,' shouted one of the Maple Leaf pranksters above the din.

The piper nodded his thanks while still playing and marching. He entered the phone booth, immediately realised where he was, and tried to turn around and march back out (still playing 'Scotland the Brave'). By this time the entire pipe band were trying to follow his example and establish some sort of record at how many pipers you could get into a phone booth. Nineteen nearly made it!

By this time the Maple Leaf Four were lying on the floor and banging the walls with their fists as the tears ran down their faces. It was bedlam but so, so funny to see.

It was a truly happy season.

Harry Broad was our musical director. He had the most delightful mini white piano in the orchestra pit and he would sit and control his band of six or seven musicians with the minimal amount of effort, the end result was always top class. You would smile down at him but you wouldn't get a flicker of reaction. Jack would often try and involve him during the show. Harry would sit as placid as you like while the audience was in stitches. But off stage, Harry was the most humorous of men and loved a gag – a musician of high quality who is, sadly, no longer with us.

Jenny Hogarth was the female part of Jack's team for this summer season; and then there were the Three Edrics (a top dancing act of two boys and a girl); and Gwen Overton and her husband Clive Stock – two very fine singers who later became good friends of mine. The Cherry Willoughby Dancers – eight girls – made up the full show, which ran for twenty-one weeks. We started in May and ended in October and did tremendous box office business. In those days people used to put their names down for any seats that might be cancelled. The box-office would be mobbed on a Monday with people literally fighting for tickets.

I remember the opening night when the after-show champagne was flowing and I found myself outside the front of the Gaiety Theatre with Jack. We were laughing and admiring the view of this famous theatre when he put his hand on my shoulder and, very seriously, said: 'Glen . . . We've made it.'

He hadn't taken his eyes off the famous façade of the Gaiety as he spoke. It was the first, and maybe the only, time I saw a sentimental Jack Milroy. We were soon back in the bar. Jack had gone down through the trap door in the floor behind the bar that led to the cellar and was bringing up more of our impresario Eric Popplewell's favourite champagne, Veuve Clicquot. Funnily enough, it was my favourite too . . . And everyone else's!

We ended our season and Eric Popplewell took the show on tour. We did four weeks back at the Tivoli Theatre, Aberdeen. Jack's wife Mary Lee, a fine performer and a star in her own right, joined us for that, and then two more weeks at the Pavilion Theatre, Glasgow followed on. We did marvellous business at every theatre and that was really the way the next few years were spent. The *Gaiety Whirl* for summer, then Dundee, Aberdeen and Glasgow Pavilion for panto, round those theatres again for short spring seasons, then summer season back at Ayr. Before I did the Ayr season of 1955, I decided my family would have a home of its own.

Today you would call it a mobile home. Then it was simply a caravan and I arranged to park it at the back of Bob McCall's garage not far from Ayr Racecourse. Bob had become a good friend to show-business folk and was a regular theatregoer at the Gaiety.

We had opened that June with an almost brand-new cast, but the atmosphere was the same – just as lively and just as fun. I was already relishing the season ahead. On 2 August I was in the theatre at 5.30 p.m. ready for a 6.30 p.m. start and was in the downstairs toilet (of all places) when I saw smoke coming under the door of my cubicle. My first reaction was that someone was playing a prank on me. I took my time coming out only to find the building really was on fire. Taking to my heels I got out as fast as I could and waited in the street, watching and disbelieving, as the fire took hold. It was a sight I will never forget – scorched forever in my memory. I felt a hand on my arm. It was Alex Munro, a Scottish comedian who had been the star comic of the 1950 *Gaiety Whirl* and also the father of film star Janet Munro. With tears in his eyes he said: 'Glen . . . It's like watching an old freen' goin' doon.'

And so it was. Thank goodness no lives were lost.

Apart from the tragedy of the theatre going up in smoke the lives of the people who worked there were in danger of going up in smoke too. The staff and artists in the *Whirl* were out of a job and the old show-business saying 'no play, no pay' came into force immediately. I had just paid cash for an Austin Atlantic car, thinking I would have the rest of the season to save some more money.

After the excitement had died down I found Beryl and Yonnie in the crowd outside the Gaiety; they had heard the news and not known if I was safe or not. We climbed into my the car and drove up to a country hostelry outside Ayr called the Hollybush Inn. We drowned our sorrows with three bags of crisps, a glass of white wine for Beryl and a beer for me. The three of us all sat there not saying a word. It was a pretty miserable party, I must say. But a good pro must always look on the bright side and keep thinking about the next opportunity. Within days I was offered a three-week run in Leith for the Edinburgh Festival along with Jack and Mary, and Gwen Overton and Clive Stock. We all jumped at the chance and this short season was an immediate success. Our new cast featured an Australian group, the Dargie Quintet; George Cormack and Irene Sharp, two very popular Scottish singers; and a new, young soprano, Patricia Bredin, who would one day be a Broadway star.

It remained a sobering experience, however, seeing the Gaiety Theatre – and, albeit temporarily, our livelihoods – reduced to ashes. We were

167

always on the lookout for ways of extending our reach. In the 1950s radio was very big and Jack Milroy decided he should get in on the act. We did a radio series on BBC Scotland Home Service called *Jack's the Boy*, produced by Iain McFadzean. Each episode was introduced by a man who was probably the best announcer BBC Scotland ever had – the legendary Bill Jack. I'm sure his voice melted the hearts of every female listener.

Jack took to the airwaves with his usual confidence. A critic gave a write-up with the headline: 'Jack's the Boy for the BBC'. It was on at 7 p.m. every Tuesday evening and the article described it as 'Light and musical, not over-weighted with sketches and not hogged by the principal'. This was after saying the programme was as good as, if not better than, *It's All Yours*. The article continued: 'The next natural steps for those in the show, Jack Milroy, Margo Henderson, new singing star Brian Douglas, the Australian Dargie Quintet, and Glen Michael, a most talented, straight man and actor, are to television.'

Indirectly, I like to think that article showed us the way.

But for a while the seasons passed very much as they had in previous years: Ayr for the summer and touring for the rest of the year. But Jack was on the ball and always looking for something that would be different on stage. He had the idea of doing take-offs of the big films and TV shows of the day, thinking they would work as first-half finales. In the *Gaiety Whirl* of 1958 we did a cracker: 'Sunday Night at the Mauchline Palladium', a complete take-off of the Bruce Forsyth show on the telly. But the one that caused me most mirth was 'The King and I'. Jack thought it would be a good idea if we broke it in at another theatre and then we could do it as a first-half finish at the Gaiety in the summer. Jack would do a take-off of Yul Brynner as the King of Siam, I was the Grand Vizier, the singer in our show took the Deborah Kerr part, and so on. Jack decided he would try it out at the Roxy, Falkirk, a theatre that was new to me.

It was only a one-night date. On the bill were two friends of ours, Dave and Joe O'Duffy, Irish and built like giants. When I saw the Roxy I was amazed at how small it was. We all had to be in one room. I couldn't call it a dressing room. We got ready for the show after having a quick run through of our The 'King and I' sketch so everyone could get some idea of what was going on. I have to say that the rehearsal didn't go very well. But we trusted in luck and everyone being good pros. It was a packed audience and the heat soon built up and continued to do so.

The show began and when it came to my entrance to do a spot with Jack, I couldn't speak. Jack looked at me as if I was daft, but all I could do was stare transfixed at the musical director who was sitting about a foot in front of me on this tiny stage. I was looking down on him and he was looking up at me smiling. I couldn't take my eyes off his head. It was bald. Except he obviously didn't want it to be, because he had painted a hairline on his bald head, either with black greasepaint or black boot polish. But what was making me wide-eyed was that the black on his head was steadily melting and running in rivulets down his face. This didn't seem to bother him one bit. He had a pint of beer on top of his piano and the audience took not one blind bit of notice. I carried on working with Jack, desperately trying not to look down in case I burst into uncontrollable laughter.

We eventually came to our 'The King and I' sketch and my black-headed friend in the pit played the opening bars of the Siamese children's entrance song; on came the O'Duffy brothers with blackout material around their shoulders representing cloaks. Underneath, they wore their outdoor clothes. They were holding two round Tennent's Lager trays, which acted as gongs. Dave hit his first. Joe was around ten seconds behind him (near enough). On came Jack as the King of Siam to roars of laughter and a round of applause. As a matter of fact, he looked quite good. From that moment on, we knew it would work. The sketch, and the night, was a success.

The show came to an end and I was going to wash my make-up off when I suddenly saw there was no washbasin. I asked Jack if there was anywhere I could wash and he said: 'Follow me.'

He had played the theatre many times in the past, of course. He led me out of the back of the theatre to a wall where there was a cold-water tap. 'There you are,' he said.

It was a bitter night. As I attempted to wash the cold water was nearly freezing onto my skin. Then I felt a slight warmness coming into the water and looking to my right I was horrified to see one of the audience standing there and relieving himself against the wall yards away from me. The high wind had blown his urine onto my face and as I looked up he said, 'Good show, Glen,' and walked away!

I'll always remember the Roxy with great affection. I was asked to compere a big-band show at the concert hall in Falkirk a couple of years ago and in one spot I asked the audience if anyone remembered the Roxy. I was amazed at how many people did. They shouted back at me with stories of the old theatre and it was great fun.

I didn't know it at the time but my days in Ayr were numbered. Jack would do the 1959 *Gaiety Whirl* and then be off to a new world. Of course, I didn't know that when we started the 1958 summer show.

We had another great cast. The Four Ramblers were our star vocal group and there was one young man in the group with a soft, Irish accent. He used to sit backstage lightly strumming on his guitar and singing to himself. He only did this at rehearsals when he wasn't in production scenes. One of the chorus girls happened to hear him and soon they were all around him asking for more of the same. The young man's name was Val Doonican. I don't know if Jack Milroy had got wind of this, or indeed, had heard him, but I know he asked Val if he would sing a solo song in the first-half finish of 'Sunday Night at the Mauchline Palladium'. Val turned him down flat, saying: 'Me, sing on my own out there? No way. I'd be petrified.'

He really was the nice, quiet, guy with cosy jumpers we all got to love on our tellies in later years.

I brought my father and mother up to Scotland from London in 1958. I thought they'd like a bit of country living in their old age. Beryl was pregnant again and we were living in a house in a lovely village outside of Ayr. Kirkmichael was a mini-Brigadoon to us and Mum and Dad loved it.

After the 1958 *Gaiety Whirl* in Ayr, Jack and I headed to the Palace Theatre, Dundee (no longer there, I'm sorry to say) to do a winter show. I was on stage the opening night of the show on 19 November and was just about to introduce Jack with: 'And now ladies and gentlemen, put your hands together, and anything else you can find, to welcome everybody's favourite—'

That was as far as I got.

Jack Milroy walked on stage with a huge smile to a tremendous round of applause. He held up his hands to quieten the audience down and said: 'It should be him you're applauding.' He turned to me and said: 'I've just taken a phone call for you. You're the father of a bouncing baby boy!'

The Palace Theatre erupted with whistles, cheers, you name it. I was flabbergasted . . . More flab than gasted I suppose, thinking back.

Jack added to my consternation by asking me in front of the packed house: 'What are you going to call him?'

'Christopher,' I replied, without any hesitation at all. He was then the patron saint of all travellers. Given the family history and our mobile home, Beryl and I thought this was very apt.

There's a very well-known saying: 'never work with children or animals'. I have worked with both for years and I can tell you it's a load of old bosh. It can be great fun and extremely amusing, like when Jack Milroy came to my office at the STV studios in Cowcaddens in Glasgow and asked me if I would be interested in doing a pantomime: *The Magic Lantern*. We'd already played nine pantos together and I was delighted to accept again. In all the previous pantos I had been the baddie but, with *Cavalcade* well established by this time, I decided I was going in as myself.

Richard O'Grady, the director of Calderpark Zoo in Glasgow, had been on *Cavalcade* many times with different animals and I had an idea about using a snake called Billy as part of my act on stage. Billy was a boa constrictor, warm to the touch and, it turned out, a great stage performer!

During the show, I would take Billy out of a box on the stage and place him around my shoulders. Almost on cue he'd wind his head round to investigate my face, flicking his long, thin tongue over my eyes, nose and mouth. This was all done very, very gently. Once satisfied that it was, indeed, me, I'd feel him relax his grip on my shoulders. If he was feeling really playful he'd wind himself right around my neck and tighten his grip on me. All I had to do was speak softly to him to say I didn't like that and he'd relax his grip. Billy understood.

I'd invite both children and adults to join me on stage to enjoy Billy's company. The kids were keen to take up the challenge of having a snake on their shoulders and Billy was always very gentle with them. They loved him. But because the adults were wary of him, Billy would sometimes play about a bit. I'm sure he had a sense of humour.

Jack Milroy hated Billy and never went near him. That surprised me because Jack had seen service in the Far East during the war. Maybe he knew of dangers that I didn't!

Richard O'Grady was very careful to see that Billy was carried back to the zoo every night by one of his staff. He was very caring with all his animals. Richard was a good professional and a good friend.

On the subject of animals and the stage, I must mention Gilbert, an eleven-year-old chimpanzee. Now, when chimps get that old, just like some elderly people, they get grumpy. And being a very large chimpanzee, he not only got grumpy, he could, if he had wanted to, given you a very nasty injury.

Gilbert was engaged as the speciality act in yet another Jack Milroy pantomime at the Pavilion Theatre in Glasgow. His trainer and owner was a Dutchman called Hans Volgebein who had trained bears for many years and had travelled the world with circus shows. Hans no longer had bears . . . he had Gilbert.

Hans would drive up to the stage door in his large American car with Gilbert sitting in the back smoking a cigar and looking like some swarthy gangster. Hans would then open the back door and Gilbert would jump out onto Hans's back. Hans had a blanket ready and he'd throw it over

Gilbert's head to cover his eyes. They would go through the stage door like that – piggyback style – and descend to their dressing room. Hans once explained to our stage manager Bryce: 'If Gilbert sees the chorus girls he gets excited and won't work.'

Bryce nodded, and with typical Glasgow humour replied: 'Aye, I've got one or two stage-hands like that. It's no' a blanket they need – it's a bucket of water.'

Gilbert had his own dressing room with a television – the only one in the whole theatre – so he could watch his favourite programmes. Hans told us he liked cowboy films and musicals. As Gilbert's dressing room was next to mine, Jack Milroy asked me if it was true Gilbert had a telly. I said yes, it was. I had sometimes seen Gilbert watching it, sitting on top of his big cage and drinking a bottle of Coke. So one night Jack asked Hans if he could watch a programme on Gilbert's television. Hans told Jack he could on the understanding that he would be out of Gilbert's dressing room before his act finished. 'Gilbert gets angry if anyone is in his room when he comes off stage,' Hans explained.

Jack agreed and waited in my dressing room until Hans and Gilbert passed my door, heading for the stage.

'On you go,' Hans shouted.

Jack was up and off and into Gilbert's dressing room as his opening music began on stage above us. I think it was *Spot the Tune* that Jack wanted to watch. I sat with him as both of us had a fairly long break before we were due back on stage. Time passed. Suddenly I was aware of loud applause and music. Gilbert had finished his act.

'Come on, Jack, that's Gilbert finished,' I said. 'You know what Hans told us.'

No reply; Jack was engrossed in his programme and oblivious to anything and everything around him.

I made for the door. 'Jack, I'm going,' I hissed as I slid out of the door and waited in my dressing-room doorway.

Gilbert passed me, hunched over Hans's shoulders. The blanket was removed and there was Jack in his dressing room. I looked on in awe: Hans stood stock-still; Jack looked like he'd just come face to face with Boris Karloff; Gilbert made a funny noise like air escaping from a steam pipe.

Hans broke the silence first. 'Jack, say something, just say something to him.'

But Jack was transfixed. Gilbert stared back at him. It was a stand-off.

'Say anything to him,' pleaded Hans, who by now had a note of panic in his voice.

Jack gulped audibly and stammered: 'I see ... I see ... you've got a telly!' And with that he gave a rather wan smile and edged warily out of the dressing room past an astonished-looking Gilbert.

17

Settling down

In 1959 my mother died from cancer which must have begun while she had been living in London. She had wonderful medical treatment in Scotland, where her illness was finally diagnosed by our GP. But sadly, the diagnosis came too late to save her.

I visited Mum the night before she died in the old Ayr County Hospital, near the railway station. As I was about to leave I said: 'I'll have to go. It'll be ringing-up time soon.'

'Oh, don't bother to ring up. I'll be OK,' Mum replied.

I told her I was talking about the curtain ringing-up at the Gaiety for the show.

We both laughed. It was the last time I saw her. She died that night. A policeman knocked at my door in Kirkmichael the following morning with the shocking news that Mum had passed away.

I played the show at the Gaiety Theatre that night. As I performed, I looked down at an empty seat in a packed house, second front row – and suddenly there was Mum, laughing away. I went cold and looked away. I looked back and she was still there. When I looked a third time there was no empty seat. A gentleman, who was laughing heartily, was sitting there. It made me think, I can tell you.

That year, 1959, was also to be my last *Gaiety Whirl*. Eric Popplewell – a humble straight man and feed – gave me a beautiful, silver cigarette box with the simple engraving: 'The Gaiety Whirl 1954 to 1959.' I still have it and treasure it, even though I haven't smoked for many, many years. It still gets a polish every day. I also see it as a dedication to Popplewell himself, a showman from Yorkshire who turned a little theatre into a place where talent could find its feet. He did a lot for Scottish entertainment.

An uncertain future turned into a delight for me. Jack Milroy was going to share the honours with Rikki Fulton at the King's Theatre in Edinburgh and star in Howard Wyndham's famous *Five Past Eight Show*. I was over the moon because I was going too. We had to find a site for the van in Edinburgh and found a lovely family at South Gyle near Corstorphine on the outskirts of Edinburgh who made us welcome on their pig farm. Mr and Mrs Gray and their daughter Elizabeth were avid theatregoers. Our daughter Yonnie attended Corstorphine Primary School and six-month-old Christopher was occasionally looked after by a superb babysitter, in the shape of a certain Miss Bates, whose claim to fame was being the nurse to the young Lord Boothby. And what a gem she was – a real nurse of the old school.

The opening of *Five Past Eight* was very exciting. Geraldo, the famous band leader, took the baton himself in the pit and conducted the orchestra for the opening night. The show did well. Rikki and Jack created Francie and Josie and performed their first sketches during that run, with Clem Ashby and Ethel Scott (Rikki's first wife) as feeds. I was supporting Jack Milroy. It was a good team effort.

Along with everyone else in the show I had to perform as required: singing, dancing and acting. It worked well for the most part. Edinburgh, I always felt, was a little reserved compared to Glasgow. The laughs in Edinburgh didn't come as easily as in Glasgow. They were more refined on the east coast while you got belly laughs in the west. Always was, and always will be like that, I think.

I was lucky to get very good producers in *Five Past Eight* and our sister show *Half Past Seven* in both Edinburgh and Glasgow. Bruce McClure was one. He was an excellent choreographer who turned into an even better producer. He became a good friend of the family and in later years STV made use of his talents. The other producer who made an impact on me was Michael Mills. What a talent he had. Michael went on to become head of comedy at the BBC in London and was responsible for the TV show *Some Mothers Do 'Ave Em*.' He made Michael Crawford a star.

Michael Mills could see talent where others would pass it by. I was in a scene with Clem Ashby, who was Rikki's feed for many years (later to be a popular announcer at STV), and two others. We had to sing a song and do a dance at the same time with specifically choreographed movements. I couldn't get it right at rehearsals and on the opening night I put one foot wrong which put Clem right off, so he got it wrong, and in the end it was a complete shambles. The King's audience in Edinburgh took it all as part of the show and cheered us to the echo. As we took our call Michael positioned himself behind the main curtain and all I could hear above the music was Michael shouting at the top of his voice: 'I won't be taking it out – you'll all bloody well learn it.'

I never did.

It was about this time that Beryl's childhood pal Betty Alberge wrote to tell her she'd got the part of the corner-shop owner Florrie Lindley in a new show on ITV called *Coronation Street*. Betty thought it might turn into something. It was an exciting time for anyone starting out in TV in those days. Betty used to come up to see Beryl and always got mobbed by people who watched *Coronation Street*. She was amazed that people called her Florrie all the time.

We used to get many famous people in to see our *Five Past Eight* or *Half Past Seven* shows. I remember going on one night at the King's, Edinburgh. During a sketch I used to take the chance to scan the audience to see if any famous faces were in. That night I wasn't disappointed. In the second row was the star of Alfred Hitchcock's film *Rebecca*, the lovely Joan Fontaine, looking even more beautiful off screen than she did on, I might add.

Our dancers were all lovely and great professionals. One I remember because she was not only a good dancer but she had an odd surname – Corbett. Margaret Corbett was a tall girl and when we were all having a snack after rehearsals at the Woodville restaurant, just up the hill from the King's, her brother Ronnie popped in for a bite. He told us that he was about to go to London to join Danny La Rue in a nightclub and thought it might be the start of something big for him.

How right he was.

As Ronnie Corbett was hoping for exciting things, so were we. In the 1960s I played everywhere and in everything, including great shows like *A Wish for Jamie*, with Jack Milroy and one my favourite artists, Fay Lenore, who did one of the best finales to a show I've ever seen. In one of the *Five Past Eight* shows she sang a song called 'The Party's Over'. Producer Bruce McClure asked her to sing it very slowly and to start it off by walking on stage on her own. At the end of a fast-moving and funny (well, most of the time) show, it's not an easy task to calm everything down. Fay did it beautifully. One by one we artists appeared to take our bows as she sang. It's a tribute to Fay's artistry that the audience refrained from applauding until the end of her song. They were spellbound. Then, when she finished, the entire theatre let rip.

That's what you call performing.

The early 1960s were busy for me with shows like *Five Past Eight, Half Past Seven* and the *Francie and Josie* television series for STV. I can remember doing the *Half Past Seven* shows at the King's in Glasgow at night and the following morning Jack Milroy, Rikki Fulton, Clem Ashby, Ethel Scott and I would be ready for rehearsals of *Francie and Josie* at the Locarno Ballroom in Sauchiehall Street.

The sad thing is that, of all the many *Francie and Josie* TV shows that we did, nothing remains on tape of the original recordings. All were destroyed in a clear-out of archives at STV many years ago. Now the only record of Rikki and Jack as Francie and Josie are clips from their stage shows which don't capture fully the wonderful magic of their earlier days.

We had a permanent TV repertory company consisting of Clem, Ethel and myself as supporting players to Jack and Rikki. The three of us played in every recording made in the *Francie and Josie* series. Dougie Murchie sometimes used to join us to play Luigi, the café owner, and, of course, we occasionally had other actors with us. Stan Mars, the writer and former stage performer, would come in now and again to write in a change of script if required, and our director Jimmy Sutherland would always be on the lookout for any extra comedy bits he spotted during rehearsals. Many a time the cry would go up: 'Keep it in.' Sometimes, even during a recording, Jack or Rikki would do an ad-lib, and that had to stay in. In those days we didn't stop the recording and do it again.

We always had a live audience and so it was treated as a stage show. What you saw was what you got. It made for a very good show. I remember in one episode Rikki was supposed to be looking out of a tenement window. There was a big close-up of him looking down as he said: 'Is that no Mrs Buckland hingin' oot?' It was an in-joke for everyone on set to enjoy as, of course, my real name is Buckland.

It's funny – people frequently still stop me in the street and talk about my *Cavalcade* TV show, but few remember me in *Francie and Josie*. I think the reason for this is that on *Francie and Josie* I was always doing the thing I loved to do the most – making myself invisible and creating another person. One week I would be an Arab chief, the next an American oil tycoon, then the boss of MI5 in a spoof spy story. Every week was a challenge and I loved it. I was always a comedy character that the two boys could feed off.

There are so many stories to tell in the making of *The Adventures of Francie and Josie*, like the time we were recording a scene where Jack and Rikki were sitting on stools in the queue waiting at the front of the Theatre Royal to get into the *One O'Clock Gang Show*. Rikki had thought it would be good for a laugh if they joined the real audience waiting to see Larry Marshall and the Gang perform live at lunchtime.

Picture the scene: Francie and Josie dressed in their familiar outfits, full stage-heavy make-up and wigs, sitting on stools in broad daylight in the middle of a very long queue of people in Cowcaddens. On the other side of the road a camera was recording every word and reaction. They both had hidden mikes on them and, amid much happy banter from the members of the queue, the floor manager called for quiet. Just as the cameras started to record on tape, a gentleman from the 'wine district' of Glasgow decided to stop and have a word with the garishly dressed twosome. Staggering up to them he cried out: 'Oh, it's the telly boys . . . All done up.' In his inebriated state, he attempted Francie and Josie's distinctive walk. The cameras were still rolling and recording every word. Rikki, not used to this sort of conversation, or behaviour, opened his mouth to say something.

Remaining completely in character, Jack stopped him and said: 'Say nothin', Josie, say nothin'.'

The drunk leered down at both of them, stared them full in the face and shouted at the top of his voice: 'Twa poofs . . . Look at their faces . . . Twa poofs,' and he wandered off to continue his lunchtime stroll.

By this time the people in the queue were all roaring with laughter. They had been entertained to a classic piece of Francie and Josie . . . Pity they could never use it! If that happened today, of course, an incident like that would be used with never a thought about who it may, or may not, offend.

The *Half Past Seven* shows at the King's Theatre in Glasgow didn't start until . . . well, I leave you to work that one out. So before I got ready at the King's I sometimes popped into another theatre in the city to see a bit of the show. The Pavilion began their first house just after 6 p.m. so one night I slipped into the early show to catch one of Scotland's characters, Lex McLean. He was a very funny man – in fact, he was a feed turned comic. After Tommy Morgan died they had had great trouble finding anyone that could fill his shoes as 'king' of the Pavilion Theatre. When Lex took over, he became the new, undisputed king.

At one time I had been asked if I would be interested in working with Lex. I thought about this as I stood at the back of the stalls watching him do his opening gags to an audience that he was holding in the palm of his hand. The laughs were coming fast and furious. I noticed a chap in front of me at the back of the stalls, on his knees laughing. He turned to me and said: 'My God, he's *so* funny.'

I looked at him and said: 'You think so?'

'Oh yes, I can't stop laughing . . . Mind you, I can't understand a word he's saying, but he's still so funny.'

This chap may not have known me, but I recognised him as he was appearing at the Alhambra Theatre, Glasgow in *Five Past Eight* at the time. It was the polished and popular comedian Dickie Henderson, who was a favourite with Glasgow audiences. Lex, of course, was very broad but he had that magic that few comedians have. He could communicate humour just by the sound of his voice.

The Pavilion Theatre, Glasgow, was always the home of variety to me after the Empire Theatre was pulled down to make way for offices. I remember walking down from the STV studios one day and bumping into a bloke as he came around the corner. Stopping in his tracks, his jaw dropped and I thought he was about to have a heart attack.

'Where is it?' he gasped.

'Where's what?' I said.

'The Empire,' he burst out.

I told him it was no longer there and, nearly in tears, he told me that he'd been abroad for about ten years and the one thing that had kept him going when he was homesick was the thought that one day he would be back and could go to the 'second-house Saturday' at the Glasgow Empire. He had his money ready in his hand, poor soul!

What a reputation the old Empire had and it's still talked about today. Stories about the first visit of Mike and Bernie Winters (a slick comedy double act, who were very popular in England) to the Empire is legendary in show business. When Mike, the suave feed, came on stage and told a few gags to start their act, he was greeted with stony silence. At his cue, Bernie, the comedian in this double act, put his head around the curtain and gave his trademark big grin to the Empire audience. They all looked back at him in total silence . . . Until a lone voice from the gallery rang out loud and clear.

'Oh my God, there are two of them!'

That got the only laugh of the act.

The Empire was known as the graveyard of many a comic, but if they liked you, you were a star. I was lucky enough to be in the Cranky series of pantomimes along with Jack Milroy as Widow Cranky at the Pavilion theatre in Glasgow for many seasons. It also saw the discovery of little Janette Anderson who, as Archie McCulloch wrote in the *Citizen* at that time, 'was a four-foot-tall, sixteen-year-old girl who stopped the show. She looked no more than ten and when she stepped forward to give a hotted-up version of "Baby Face" she had a great reception.'

Janette was one of Widow Cranky's children and it started her on the road to fame as another 'Cranky' – Jimmy Kranky, of course. It was 'fandabidozi', all right!

Archie was kind enough to give me a mention in that same write-up: 'Looking over the cast I still think that Glen Michael is the most talented feed in the business.'

And I never paid Archie a penny!

I was beginning to get noticed a little and as I did summer seasons in Glasgow and Edinburgh with Jack Milroy and also *Francie and Josie*, life was getting very busy. Before I knew it, it was 1965, and I was at the Alhambra Theatre in Glasgow in *Five Past Eight*. Jack and Rikki were starring and doing their Francie and Josie characters in one section of the show as usual.

I remember a scene where we had five white grand pianos coming up from the bowels of the theatre on a lifting stage with Rikki on the main piano in the centre playing 'Rhapsody in Blue'. Now, Rikki didn't read a note of music, but he was a wonderful pianist who played everything by ear. On the opening night this scene stopped the show.

I'll always remember the Alhambra season of 1965 because it changed my life. Towards the end of our run I was in Jack's dressing room. For some reason we were looking at some old photographs spread out on the floor when Jack suddenly said, very quietly: 'I'm thinking of going to London.'

My first reaction was: 'Well, I don't want to go. I'm happy here.'

Jack continued: 'I'd like to try and see what the London scene is like.'

Then it clicked. He was trying to tell me, gently, that he was going to London on his own. At that very moment I had a feeling of panic. It was as if a marriage had ended. I had taken the last thirteen years for granted. Jack looked a little sad, I thought. I think he wanted to try something different and maybe he was right.

Jack said he would try to get me a job somewhere. It was meant kindly, I know, but I said not to bother because I would like to try and make it on my own too. There were no angry scenes or bad feelings, just an emptiness and a kind of void for the rest of that season. I'd spent a large portion of my professional career as right-hand man to Jack Milroy. We'd gone from the Victory Theatre, Paisley, to national television. It was a long journey and one I will never forget nor regret. And, of course, it led me to meet a man I'm proud to have called a friend: Rikki Fulton.

Some people used to think Rikki was a bit standoffish in his personal life. But in actual fact Rikki could be the kindest and most thoughtful of people at work and play. He had a reputation of not liking children – well, badly behaved ones. I can only speak from my own experience and that is to say that he was kindness itself to both of my two children, Yonnie and Chris.

On a dinner date at Rikki's house in Glasgow, Ethel, Rikki's first wife, served some soup into which she had added a rather liberal amount of brandy. Chris, who was about six at that time, had to leave the table suddenly after eating as the soup was just too rich for him. Ethel simply hadn't thought that the 'dash' of alcohol might not suit a child's palate! Before anyone could do anything, Chris dashed out of the dining room but didn't make it to the downstairs toilet and was violently sick on the

Fulton's spotless, cream carpet – right behind Rikki's much-loved grand piano. Momentarily, Beryl and I were mortified, but Rikki was first up to help Chris and to ensure that he didn't get upset at what had just happened. Chris was tearful and embarrassed, Rikki was so kind to him.

Rikki and I used to play the odd round of golf together at Balmore near Glasgow and one day as we tried to get out of our umpteenth bunker, he brought up the fact that I was still living in a caravan. Was it good for the kids? Didn't Beryl find it hard to cope, living in a caravan with a family?

I tried to explain that it was because we wanted to be together as a family that we had chosen the nomad life – at least when I toured from theatre to theatre we could all be together in our own wee home. I forgot all about this conversation until, one day, I had a phone call at the caravan site in Stepps in Glasgow. We were based there whenever I worked in the city. We had no phone ourselves but Rikki had left a message asking me to ring him.

I did so and he was a bit short with me saying he would like me to meet him at his bank in Byres Road in Glasgow, as he wanted me to sign something. I said I would. Rikki set the time and the following morning at 11 a.m. I arrived at his bank. I was shown into the manager's office and Rikki and his bank manager were sitting waiting for me. After handshakes all round Rikki said, quite bluntly: 'Sign that, will you, Glen?'

The manager pushed a sheet of paper across the desk towards me. Now, I never sign anything until I read what it's all about and this was no exception. I started to read it and realised it was an agreement: Rikki was standing as a guarantor for me at the bank and I was to get as much money as I needed to buy a house or a flat. Flabbergasted, I looked across the room at Rikki who burst out laughing and said: 'Well, you'll never do it on your own.'

I shook hands with him and said not a word of thanks – I was far too choked up with unexpected emotion. Indeed, I think I shook hands with everyone – including the tellers – on my way out of the bank and literally sailed back on cloud nine to the caravan to tell Beryl our great and unexpected news.

We bought a lovely, three-bedroom flat in Falkland Mansions in Hyndland in Glasgow's West End.

And all thanks to Rikki Fulton.

18

A new direction

It was 1966 – a year not best loved in Scotland for certain sporting reasons – and it marked a new dawn in my career. Michael Mills, our *Five Past Eight* producer in Edinburgh, was now head of comedy at the BBC; he contacted me and invited me to go down to London for a television recording of *The World of Wooster* starring Ian Carmichael and Dennis Price. I was thrilled.

Arriving in London on the first day of rehearsals I was introduced to Ian and Dennis. I found them to be delightful and very friendly.

Michael took me to one side at the reading – something I found very strange. 'Glen,' he said, 'I don't want to put you off but you're playing a scout master in this episode and, please, no funny walks, no funny glasses on the end of your nose, and no farting. This is comedy, not farce.'

For a second I was taken aback. Then I looked at him again and he broke into a huge grin. He was joking, of course. Michael was an excellent producer – he knew if I got the chance I'd try and build up my part in my own way, not his. We had a week's rehearsal and then we recorded it. It all went well and after the recording Michael asked me what I was doing next. I told him I was going back to Scotland.

'Don't go. Stay here and you'll get plenty of work,' he said.

Michael tried to change my mind a few times but I told him I was hoping for things to turn up in Scotland.

I arrived back in Glasgow for a meeting with Jimmy McNair, a great writer who worked for STV in Glasgow at that time. He was also one half of a partnership that used to write pantomimes for the Pavilion Theatre. Jimmy tracked me down and asked me what I was doing. I said I had a 'little of this and a little bit of that', which didn't raise a flicker of a smile with Jimmy. He said there was a chance of me presenting a television programme. Would I be interested?

I got serious and asked what he was talking about.

'Be here tomorrow at ten in the morning and try to learn a story off by heart. You could be in line to present a children's programme.'

I had a few children's books at home that I read to Yonnie and Chris. I noticed one on the shelf called *Sam the Pig*. I thought it looked just the job. That night I lay in bed reading and I picked on a part of the story I thought I could memorise by the next day. The following morning I presented myself at STV studios – the Theatre Royal, as it was then. Jimmy met me and took me up to a tiny studio no larger than a telephone box. Later, they told me that it was the continuity announcer's studio.

Jimmy introduced me to the sound engineer and, after telling me he had to be at a meeting, he left. I was in a chair with a small desk in front of me, and on the desk was a microphone. Facing me, about a foot away, was a TV camera. The soundman set the mike up to his satisfaction and said: 'Good luck.' I was on my own with a head full *Sam the Pig* in a tiny room with four blank walls and Big Brother staring at me, ready to record.

The voice of the engineer came out of the ether.

'Ready when you are.'

I wished I had sneaked that little book *Sam the Pig* in with me. Could I reproduce what I had memorised?

The voice broke into my thoughts again.

'Ready when you are . . .' it said, again, a little impatient this time.

So I started. I looked at the camera and tried to smile.

'Hello,' I said. 'I'd like to tell you a story. It's about a friend of mine called Sam the Pig.'

Then my mind went blank. Panic set in. I started to perspire, my voice went up a notch, and I just knew I was smiling too much.

'This pig was very intelligent . . .'

I thought I'd got back on track but, no, I'd lost the place again. I carried on making it all up as I went along. I have no idea what gibberish I was talking. I was sure it must have been awful to listen to. Afterwards I thought I'd been in that sweat-hole for an hour but I was only recording for four minutes. I couldn't think of anything else to go on with so I said, 'The End.'

I laughed and smiled again.

'Is that it?' asked the sound engineer.

Did I notice a 'thank God that's over' tone in his voice?

I came out of the tiny studio and said thank you to the sound man, who responded with a smile and a nod. I left and walked down the stairs and out of the Theatre Royal. There was a pub next door in those days called The Top Spot. I made right for it. I had a large whisky and sat in a corner of the bar feeling very down. I'd botched it. I was the only one in the bar and I was glad of that, as I was in no mood to talk.

I don't know how long I was there but the door opened and in came Jimmy McNair.

'Where've you been? We've been searching all over for you,' he almost shouted. I told him to sit down as the barman was looking a bit upset at the way he'd dashed in.

Jimmy sat down beside me and told me in a low tone that Francis Essex wanted to see me. I laughed. Why would the controller of programmes want to see me after that shambles of a performance?

Jimmy said: 'You'd better get up there quick.'

'Up there' meant the corner room, first floor, which looked onto Hope Street and Cowcaddens. I made my way past security on the front door, up the stairs, and into the outer office, where a very pleasant young lady escorted me into the presence of STV's controller of programmes, Francis Essex: the big man.

189

When I say 'big man', I describe the position he held rather than his stature. Francis Essex was actually a small, stocky man, but he knew the television game like the back of his hand. Francis said he had watched my efforts in the tiny studio. I started to say how sorry I was for making such a mess of it. Much to my surprise he waved my apologies to one side and told me that forgetting my lines didn't worry him. He liked the way I attacked the camera and had smiled and laughed my way through it.

I was astounded; I barely noticed that he was offering me a job. He said it might be only for five weeks then we'd see. I was told they had some cartoons in the building and they thought it might be a good idea to do a cartoon programme for children. Would I present it? There was no budget and all STV could offer would be £14 a programme. I accepted.

In an instant, *Glen Michael's Cartoon Cavalcade* was born.

And from small acorns, mighty oak trees grow. It started out as a simple introduction by me of Bugs Bunny, Sylvester the Cat or any cartoon that happened to be around. Slowly it evolved into something much more. We added birthday announcements, used bluescreen so I could walk into cartoons and join the action, invited star guests and even went out and about filming mini comedy-dramas of our own. There were spin-offs like the *Cavalcade* Road Show, and we added characters like Totty the Robot, Rusty and Rudi (our very own TV dogs) and finally, the biggest star of them all, Paladin – the only talking lamp in television.

We started with an editor, a bundle of cartoons, and me. The editor was John Fletcher and he just happened to be a film buff. John loved films from as far back as he could remember, and as a young lad he used to be a film-winder in the projection box at the Ionic Cinema in Golders Green. At the end of each performance he'd finish his winding and dash to the next cinema with the huge rolls of film on his bike. It was only after working with John for many years, and quite by chance during a conversation, that we discovered I had been sitting in that very cinema at that very same time, watching those films that he had been winding and running about the city with on his bicycle. It's a small world.

190

John and I used to sit for hours on end looking at cartoons and editing them if they needed it. We made a rule: if there was a fight scene in a cartoon it had to have a funny ending. Violence, except in a cartoon way, was out. I have always held the view that children know the difference between real violence and cartoon knockabout.

John worked with me for twenty-six years and we never had a cross word that entire time. It was such fun to go to work every day. People used to think I popped onto the screen on a Friday, Saturday or Sunday and just said, 'Here's a cartoon.' That *is* actually how it started out, but it quickly snowballed from those simple beginnings into a production everyone in the studio wanted to get involved in. It was a very happy show.

But it's funny how time has changed the industry. I was amazed the last time I recorded a spot in a television studio. I was asked to sit in a chair by the producer and he sat facing me with a cameraman and a camera at his side. A sound man was fiddling away at a portable machine. 'Speak up please,' he asked politely. Looking at him, I realised he had worked on *Cavalcade* many times. The hair was a little greyer, there were a few more lines on his face, but he was the same nice guy. Then it hit me. This was it and, with apologies to Jerome K. Jerome, it was 'Three Men and a Camera', and nothing else in the studio.

'Where is everybody?' I asked.

I was told that this was as good as it got. I thought it must be lonely for a newsreader reading autocue from a robotic camera operated from a control room. There were no stage-hands and no feeling of life. My first thought was that they'd taken away the lifeblood of entertainment. The soul has gone out of television. I even remember feeling like that on the last recording I did of *Cavalcade*. They tried a robot camera on me and although it had my autocue on it, seeing it move without a human behind it sent a shiver up my spine. This shiver had a voice and it was saying to me: 'You've had the best days, old mate. It's downhill from here. Dr Who is the new controller of television.'

Maybe it removes human error, but human error is what gives broadcasting a personality. There was one episode of *Cavalcade* where everyone was a little late in preparing for the show. I was late in make-up, the director's PA had trouble parking her car, and to top it all Rusty wanted a pee just as I was ready to go into the studio. It was just one of those days.

Even the lady at the autocue was a little late coming into the studio and setting up her machine. She arrived out of breath and quickly threaded what looked to my untrained eye to be mini toilet rolls with writing on into her machine. But it wasn't graffiti – it was my script, all neatly typed and large enough so that I could see what I had to say from a few feet away. We had been doing *Cavalcade* for years at this point and people were very relaxed on the studio floor. Most of the crew knew the routine of the show backwards. In fact, many of them said they could do it in their sleep. I always said to them: 'Be prepared, there's always the unexpected. Be complacent and television will attack you and kill you stone dead when you least expect it.'

'Action,' called the director and the recording began with 'Day Out', the *Cavalcade* signature tune. (That signature tune is very distinctive and happy. I discovered it while searching through the commercial recording section at STV in 1966. It was written by Johnny Hawksworth, who also penned the theme tunes for TV sitcoms *George and Mildred* and *Man About the House*, and also incidental music for the 1967 *Spider-Man* cartoon. To this day people still whistle it at me when they see me in the street. After the first show many people asked me if I wanted to change it but I didn't. I instinctively felt it was so right) I was sat at my usual place at the desk with Rusty sitting on top of it close beside me. I smiled broadly and began to read.

'Good evening,' I began with great conviction – even though I knew the programme was going out at 2.30 p.m. the following Sunday afternoon. 'Are you sad this Sabbath Day? Do you feel the world has forgotten you? Fear not. Today I have a story of hope for you . . . Jesus says . . .'

At that point I stopped talking.

There was complete silence and even the stage-hand at the back of the studio stopped reading the football pages. The floor manager swiftly walked over to me and with great concern said, 'Are you alright, Glen?'

Rusty growled at him and the director's voice came over on the floor speaker: 'Why have you stopped, Glen?'

'Because I'm reading the bloody *Late Call* – that's why!' I shouted back.

Everyone fell about laughing. They hadn't been listening to a word I'd been saying and even the girl operating the autocue hadn't twigged. It had all been a mix-up, of course. In all the rush, had simply picked up the wrong roll from the desk. That was how *Late Call* appeared on *Cavalcade* for the first and last time.

At the start of *Cavalcade*, Jimmy McNair wrote the script, or what little there was of it. He also came up with the idea for the WOOF (World Organisation of Fidos) Club'. STV produced *The Glen Michael Cavalcade Annual* every year and one of the things you could do was fill in a form in the book and become a member. The only rule was that you had to be kind to animals and it had to be signed by a parent or adult in the family. You got a WOOF badge by return.

The books were designed and drawn by Rod McLeod, a very talented cartoonist. His strip cartoons of Rudi and Casper, Sherlock Haggis and Dr Neeps were all very good. I wrote stories like Tomboy Trudy, and Old Ebeneezer, about an old nightwatchman from the days when you had men like him to guard holes in the road that had been dug up. He told stories to pass the night away and these were mysteries that the kids loved. The rest of the book would be of general interest to children of primary-school age.

At the start of *Cavalcade*'s long run it only took a day to record so I could do other work. Like I did in 1965 for Jimmy Logan. My first love had always been the theatre, and the year before I started in television with my own show, Jimmy asked me if I would be interested in doing a comedy play at his own theatre, the Metropole (originally the old

Empress) at St George's Cross in Glasgow. STV had asked him to record a series of nine shows there to be called the *Jimmy Logan Theatre Hour*, which were to be broadcast over the winter months.

I appeared in *Friends and Neighbours* among an impressive cast that included Jimmy himself (of course), Walter Carr, Paul Young and Myra Forsyth, and which was directed by the great Jimmy Sutherland, who directed all the Francie and Josie TV series. *Friends and Neighbours* was screened on TV in two parts – 'Co-existence' on channel 10 at 10.15p.m. on 21 November 1965 and 'Join the Party' on 28 November – and was a great success.

I worked a lot with Jimmy, including a double-act at the City Varieties Theatre in Leeds for the popular TV show *The Good Old Days*.

Quite by chance I met Jimmy Logan on the train from Ayr to Glasgow one day. He'd been visiting Culzean Castle and checking on the apartment that he had there at that time. During our conversation Jimmy asked me if I would be interested in doing a play he was presenting called *One for the Pot*.

He had Stanley Baxter lined up for the lead and that fine actor Phil McCall, whom I later worked with in the *Over to Una* television series. My part was to be the butler who likes a dram of whisky now and again. Right up my street!

We did a successful tour of *One for the Pot*, and I remember playing at His Majesty's Theatre, Aberdeen. I had to dash on and say my line to Stanley. I forget what it was but Stanley than came back with a funny line that always got a big roar of laughter. Then the curtain would descend to massive applause. Now, you have to understand one thing about Stanley Baxter: he is a perfectionist. Everything has to be right, absolutely perfect, and nothing else will ever do. I was standing at the side of the stage waiting for my cue when a stage-hand started talking to me about the old days when I performed with Jack Milroy at the Tivoli Theatre. I was trying to listen for my cue and not be rude to the stage-hand. Suddenly, there was a silence in the theatre. It's not like any other silence. It's as if the whole world has stopped. The stage-hand stopped speaking to me and, looking over my shoulder and onto the stage he said, very quietly: 'I think you're on!' I turned to see Stanley, centre stage, glaring off stage, and into the wings at me.

I dashed on, said my line, Stanley said his. Silence. The curtain came down, not to laughter and applause, but to the sound of squeaks and grinds from supporting wires.

I apologised immediately to Stanley and he was very understanding. I could see he was furious, just as I would have been in his position. His timing had been ruined by my inattention. In comedy, timing is everything. One split second too late – as I had been – or early and the whole caboodle is shot.

Stanley was wonderful to work with both on stage and in television. I worked with him under David Bell's direction for the BBC. David was a remarkable and clever producer and director. I recall doing some outside filming at Jordanhill. A lady had agreed to her house being used for filming and Stanley had an idea about him and me flying out of the front room of this house. Trouble was the window was too small for us both to get through.

'No problem,' said David Bell. 'We'll take the window out.'

It was a lovely, traditional, house and, as it was, the lady already had all her furniture in the front garden. But David would never let a little thing like a window stop a production of his from going ahead. The bemused lady was assured her window would be replaced at the expense of the BBC. Two carpenters, who were on standby on the set, quickly went to work and the entire bay window was removed as she looked on in horror.

Meanwhile, Stanley and I got ready to do the gag. It required both of us to dive out of the window at the same time and land in a dustbin together with our bottoms facing the camera. But having done stunts and falls all my life, I really didn't fancy doing this one. I told Stanley he could do it, but I wouldn't. I don't think Stanley was very pleased, though much to my surprise he didn't say anything. I'd been thinking that both of us could injure our backs if we did the stunt. But brave man that he is, Stanley did it – and he *did* hurt his back at the same time! The show must go on . . .

The carpenters put in a new window before you could say 'double glazing' but the costs must have given the BBC accountants palpitations. That was the Stanley Baxter way: only the best, no matter what it cost. Of course, he was absolutely right.

19

Golf with James Bond

I hoard things from the past, and that includes letters. I came across one the other day from Peter Sellers asking me to try to find out if there were any former RAF Gang Show members in Scotland and, if there were, would I let him know as he was trying to organise a reunion dinner at the Dorchester Hotel in London. Peter also sent me a lapel badge in enamel with the words 'Gang Show' supported by wings on it – I still have it.

Those were the days when he was a nice, gentle guy – the Peter I like to remember. Over the years I kept in touch with him but you could tell, as time passed, the changes that were taking place in his personality.

Of course, people do change. One such person I can recall was a gentleman who went by the name of Bing Hitler; he was a stand-up comedian of some note a few years ago in Scotland. He used to take the mickey out of me in his stage act. He was a guest on one of my outside broadcasts at the Tron Theatre and is now known as Craig Ferguson. He is doing very well indeed as a talk-show host in America – a real star. In the same *Cavalcade* recording was another young man trying to make his way in the theatre. At the Tron he was in panto, performing in skirts as a dame. His name was Alan Cumming.

I remember Craig and I having a conversation about comedy and he said he didn't know which direction to go in next. In fact, he was looking for some advice. I told him he couldn't do much better than copy Jack

Milroy and Rikki Fulton. It was their timing and sheer force of personality that could teach young, aspiring comics the way to handle an audience – just as Craig is doing now, in fact.

Over the years many people appeared on *Cavalcade* who went on to become big stars. One pop group called Slick appeared on *Cavalcade*, eager to talk about their new record. One member of the band simply wouldn't open his mouth. He just sat and smiled. I got the shock of my life recently when I saw him cooking on television and having no difficulty in talking to camera. That's something I'd never have believed possible of the mute boy who became the pop star Midge Ure. I remember being invited to see the band's stage act at the old Apollo Theatre, opposite the Pavilion Theatre, Glasgow. It used to be Green's Playhouse in an earlier life, and it was packed to the ceiling. When they played the sound was deafening. I bounced up and down in my seat in the box – but I wasn't doing the bouncing. The audience were jumping up and down so much that the whole theatre was actually pulsating, and it was as if the balcony were on springs. It frightened the life out of me, so much so that was the first and last pop concert I ever attended! They were a very good act though.

We had all sorts of guests on *Cavalcade*. I thought it would be a good idea to get one of Radio Clyde's well-known presenters on to let the people see the face behind the voice. I had joined Radio Clyde in 1974 when it was first set up at the invitation of their then head of entertainment, Andy Park. Andy wrote in his introduction to the station: 'Each presenter has an attitude and a style that is his own and the result is a series of daytime programmes which exceeds in its breadth and variety the output of any other station on air in Britain.' The important part of that statement is *each presenter has an attitude and a style* – a must for the listener, I think.

In the end we had twenty faces behind the voices – like the witty, if irreverent, Frank Skerret with his Wednesday night musical memories show; Tiger Tim Stevens (still going strong today) with his 8.30 p.m.

Thursday night *Sounds New Show*; then the 10.30 p.m. news; and then it was my *Middle of the Road Music Show* from 10.35 p.m.

I remember the first time I was on air – live of course. The announcer finished the news and said: 'And now *Middle of the Road Music*. It's over to Glen Campbell!'

My opening music played and I came on air to say: 'This is not Glen Campbell . . . But I wish I had his money.' I must say I enjoyed every moment of my six years at Radio Clyde.

The Clyde presenter I eventually asked to come on *Cavalcade* was Richard Park, now a big name in entertainment after becoming 'head teacher' in TV's popular *Fame Academy*. Back then he was a shy, tall, long-haired, guy with very thick horn-rimmed glasses.

Around the time *Cavalcade* first started in 1966, we had moved to Prestwick, where we had bought a nice three-bedroom semi-detached house. I still have the bill for removals from Hyndland in Glasgow to Prestwick, Ayrshire. Included in the price were the services of three men who had to bring our furniture down three flights of stairs, travel to Prestwick and unload. The cost: £32 and 10 shillings. I wonder how much it would be today.

We hadn't been in Prestwick long when I received a phone call from Rikki Fulton asking me if he could come down and play a round of golf with me at Prestwick Old Course. Naturally I said I'd be delighted. Rikki asked if he could bring a couple of old pals with him and I, once again, said of course he could (although my one worry was paying for all of us at the course! Money was a little tight at the time if I remember . . .).

The day duly came and a knock at the door heralded their arrival. I opened the door and Rikki stepped into the house followed by his two companions. Into our small living room stepped Rikki, Iain Stewart and Sean Connery. In 1966 Sean Connery was at the height of his James Bond fame, having already completed filming *Dr No*, *From Russia With Love*, *Goldfinger* and *Thunderball*. And there he was standing in my wee living room in Prestwick. Iain Stewart I knew from the Saints and Sinners Club and the Royal and Ancient – where he was later to become president. A philanthropist and well-known industrialist, Iain received a knighthood in 1968. To my relief, paying for the round had been taken out of my hands as Iain had contacted the club and, I presume, 'made arrangements'.

We were going to tee off at 2 p.m. It was just after 12.30 p.m. so I suggested there were two options. We could go to the club or a hotel and get something to eat or we could have a bite to eat at my home. We all looked at each other and I said that if we stayed it would be a bit primitive, as we hadn't unpacked everything from our recent move. Sean was the first to break the embarrassed silence.

'If it's all the same to you, I'd like to eat here as I'm a bit fed up of hotel food and I'd love some home cooking.'

I was pleased and Beryl was delighted – she had made roast beef and Yorkshire pudding just in case Rikki and his guests had decided to stay. We all sat around our dining table eating with knives and forks that didn't match and no tablecloth. Having said that, everyone, including Sean, thoroughly enjoyed the meal and it was such a good laugh.

After lunch we left the house and made for the golf course. One or two neighbours had realised by then who our guest was and couldn't resist peeking through their net curtains at 007 as he got into Rikki's car.

Our round of golf was certainly interesting. We were a foursome and I was first to hit the ball. To say I was nervous would be an understatement. I placed the ball down, conscious of all the eyes on me – not only from my fellow players but also from the clubhouse, the kitchens and the houses overlooking the course. Everyone seemed to know that James Bond himself was playing Prestwick Old Course.

Those who know that wonderful course won't need to be told that the first fairway runs alongside the main railwayline to Glasgow. In fact, Prestwick station is right beside the clubhouse. I got my trusty 3 wood out and tried to look confident. I must say I hit the ball with a sound that would have done justice to the one o'clock gun going off in far-away Edinburgh. The flight of the ball was another matter. All four of us watched in fascination as it made a graceful arc that took it way to my right, just as a railway engine pulling a line of empty coal wagons was passing on its way north. We all heard the 'plop' as my ball came to rest in the last truck. Stunned silence – no one said a thing. We watched the train disappear into the horizon with my ball. Rikki took off his cap off, as if a well-loved friend had died and, with real envy in his voice, intoned, just like the Rev. I.M. Jolly: 'Glen, that'll be the longest drive today!'

Iain and I were playing Rikki and Sean. Sean was last to play and I don't think he'd been playing very long at that time because he took a long time to do everything 'correctly' – the feet, the grip, the wiggle-waggle of the bum. It was all there. Sean was going through that routine when a small boy ran up to him on the ninth tee and asked: 'Are you James Bond?'

Sean smiled and said: 'Yes.'

With a huge and cheeky grin on his face the youngster replied: 'I think you're rotten.'

And then he ran away, laughing.

Actually, we were all laughing – and none more so than Sean himself.

We had great fun but it was not the best golf. We returned to my house and after a glass of refreshment I asked them what they'd like to do now – go out to a hotel or stay at my home.

Sean was the first to say he'd like to stay where he was as he was on a diet and, again, really didn't want to eat any more hotel food. Beryl served him some of her wonderful homemade cake, which he ate with relish along with a cup of tea.

It was at that point our teenage daughter Yonnie slipped into the room. She and her brother Chris had spent some considerable time on our stairs peering in to see 007. Once they realised who our famous guest was they had been sworn to secrecy but were bursting to tell their pals. Sean had spotted them and given a broad sideways wink at them both, acknowledging their quiet presence. This act prompted Yonnie's arrival into the room but Chris was too overawed and stayed where he was, still watching and listening to the conversation. Yonnie sat quietly at the edge of the sofa, not quite believing that the world's biggest heart-throb was a few feet away from her.

Sean asked her how old she was and when she nervously replied, 'I've just turned fifteen,' he put his hand in his pocket and drew out a fiver as a belated birthday present. Yonnie, by now completely red-faced and nonplussed, promptly refused to take it, saying her birthday had been a few weeks ago and it wouldn't be right to accept it as he was a guest. Sean just smiled, understanding the effect he was having on an excited teenager, and replaced the note in his pocket.

You can imagine the reaction my pair must have had at school the next day. It went something like this: 'Sean Connery was in my house yesterday!'

'Aye, that'll be right, big heid.'

Our Prestwick home was a happy meeting place for many of my show-business colleagues at that time. Moira Anderson, an Ayrshire lass; Johnny Beattie, a much-liked Scots comic and now *River City* soap star; and Australian comedian Dick Bentley, to mention only a few. Dick was a star of the smash-hit radio show *Take it from Here* and was guesting on the Una McLean TV show, *Over to Una* (which I was also working on at the time). Una has always been a great performer.

Over the years, *Cavalcade* became involved in many activities outside the TV studios. For instance, I had columns for the *Sunday Mail*, the *Ayrshire Post* and the *Edinburgh Evening News*. Under the *Cavalcade* banner we tried to communicate with primary-school children across Scotland by encouraging them to participate in all manner of things.

We also worked with Yorkhill Hospital in Glasgow. The *Daily Record* of 31 January, 1981 ran the story a young boy called Mark being hit by a car and left in a coma. I was asked if I would record a tape that they could play to him, as he was a huge fan of the show. I can't tell you how happy all the *Cavalcade* team were when we learned shortly after that he'd come out of his coma. I was delighted to have the lad in the studio some time later to wish him luck along with Paladin and Rusty. We did a few recordings just like that during the life of the show and it was always a pleasure to try to help in any way that we could.

On a lighter side, in the 1990s the *Sunday Mail* took a poll among Scotland's kids nominating the 'prize guys' on TV. Top spot went to Philip Schofield. I came eighth, beating Bill Cosby and Bruce Forsyth, who were placed ninth and tenth. Guess who beat me into seventh place? Edd the Duck!

20

The Cavalcade continues

My first *Cavalcade* contract was for one year. Francis Essex, the controller of programmes at STV asked his number two, David Johnston, to come into his office and we all shook hands on it. Little did I know that I would have to wait until each succeeding year to have the contract confirmed for the following season. The same routine continued for twenty-six years.

But first time round I can remember driving back down to Prestwick and singing all the way. I was delighted as it meant I could do *Cavalcade* and still work on other things like radio and stage – although appearing on BBC Television as well was a no-go area in those days.

As we moved into the 1970s, *Glen Michael's Cavalcade* was born. It was about this time I started to think we had to do a bit more than introduce cartoons and read out birthday greetings. I decided we would have to get out and about and do some filming for the show. Although *Cavalcade* was a children's show I also wanted the whole family to become more involved. I'd noticed that the letters coming into the show asking for a birthday mention were not only from children, but also from Mum and Dad and other grown-up members of the family.

I decided to encourage everyone to be a bit more ambitious in their letters and told them to include a photo or make them artistic. It started to mushroom and I used to get security vans arriving at the studio laden with all sorts of letters, one of which still sticks vividly in my memory. The film *Jaws* had just been released into the cinemas and was all the rage. One day the security van delivered a birthday card that was made of wood and was about three feet long and one foot wide. The flat surface was painted blue and white to represent sea waves and in bold relief was a perfect carving of a shark rearing out of the water with its jaws wide open. Inside its mouth was a balloon caption wishing one young viewer a very happy birthday. It was really wonderful and clever.

There were so many items like that and the response became so good that I had to be given a special room under a staircase at STV for storage. I ended up with a room stuffed full of these items. Sad to say, I eventually had to let them all go because STV needed the space . . .

I had three very good directors who used to take it in turns to do my show: Ted Williamson, Dermott McQuarry and Geoff Rimmer. Sometimes Don Cumming or John McDonald, also both excellent directors, might take over. Our production week for *Cavalcade* started with me arriving at the studios to view and edit the cartoons. As I said, John Fletcher – my editor – and I were very strict about the content of each cartoon. If we were uneasy about anything at all, be it violence, racism or innuendo of any kind, we moved on and looked at the next cartoon. We did show a cartoon character you might remember called Pepé Le Pew, a cute wee skunk who was always chasing after girls and making comic remarks that were funny to adults, but not so much for the children. After a few transmissions I called a halt to this cartoon. Yes, it was comedy, but the wrong kind of comedy for the kids. The truth is I was uneasy and so it was out.

Another problem we encountered was a Bugs Bunny cartoon made during World War II. The story had Bugs in the army, deep in the jungle, and it made fun of the Japanese in a nasty way – the comedy lines were so racist. I binned it there and then and I believe the distributors eventually destroyed it.

It was a long process looking at cartoons and then making a shortlist of the ones we thought would make up a balanced programme. Over the years, although we usually had a variety to choose from times we felt we were scraping the bottom of the barrel. Supply was always a problem and it was suggested we use Eastern European cartoons. Artistically they were very good, but as comedy cartoons they were dreadful for our viewers. The humour is so different and the kids would simply have switched off in droves. They wanted Spider-Man, Casper the Friendly Ghost, Road Runner, Foghorn Leghorn, Sylvester the Cat, Tweety Pie, and fun, fun, fun, all the way.

I remember getting hold of *Spider-Man* for the first time. It was like finding gold. The children went crazy for every action-packed episode. We just couldn't get enough to supply the demand. You know, I hear so many people saying the children of today are so much more sophisticated than the children of the 1970s and '80s. If that's so, how come one of the biggest cinema box-office successes in the twenty-first century is – wait for it – *Spider-Man*!

I have been working with primary-school children since the 1960s and the good news is that they are the same today as they were back then. The great thing about children is they have no hang-ups about age. I've played hundreds of primary schools over the last forty years, and when they see me at the end of a show the phrase they often use when they talk to me is: 'You're cool!' They simply couldn't care less about how old you are in calendar years. If you're fun, you're fun, and if you entertain them and make them laugh they really appreciate it. Mind you, sometimes one wee boy or girl will ask how old I am. They couldn't care less; it's usually Mum or Dad who wants to know. I always say: 'I'm 104.' That sends them away laughing and giggling.

I'm still often stopped in the street with questions about *Cavalcade*. In fact, if I'm not smiled at and gently reminded of my TV show at least five times a day, I get quite annoyed. The questions are mostly about Rusty, Paladin or me. So perhaps it might be a good idea to set one or two things straight here and now.

Dogs first.

There were three incarnations of Rusty – Rusty, Rudi, and Casper. Rusty Number One was a lovely, blonde, wire-haired standard dachshund. Unlike *Blue Peter*, Rusty was a true pet who lived in our family home. We had bought him from a kennel in Yorkshire that had been recommended to us. In fact, we bought all our dogs from the same kennel except for two, which came from a kennel in Kirkintilloch. Rusty Number One was our first TV dog and highly intelligent. When you met his gaze you got a feeling he just *knew* what you were thinking. Francis Essex had warned me not to use an animal every week on television and only to use him now and again. I ignored his advice when I saw the reaction that Rusty's appearances were getting from the children by their letters and phone calls. Many children didn't have a dog, or couldn't have one for some reason or another.

Unfortunately Rusty died at the early age of seven. He developed a problem with his kidneys that we, at first, thought had been rectified after he underwent an operation. Sadly, though, he became very ill.

During this period we decided to buy Rudi, a standard, dark-haired, smooth dachshund. I knew how dreadfully Rusty would be missed and wanted to introduce another pet before the inevitable happened so the children wouldn't become too upset. Of course, all the while we desperately hoped that Rusty would overcome his kidney problems.

One day, shortly before he died, Yonnie came home from school and pushed open the living-room door. Rusty was behind the door and by opening it she had knocked him clean over. She told me later she'd burst into tears as she'd obviously hurt him as his tummy was, by then, quite swollen with his kidney problems. Rusty had looked up at her with the most doleful expression. The two locked eyes and she swore that Rusty was trying to tell her that it was alright, he knew she hadn't meant to hurt him. Soon after that I had to take Rusty to our vet in Troon for yet another operation. That evening I got a phone call from the vet telling us the dreadful news. Rusty had died peacefully, but my family were inconsolable.

Rudi was a delight to have as a pet. He was gentle and hated the rain. When we got him I thought it would be a good idea if the boys and girls could have a feeling of owning him from afar, as it were. I asked them to send in their ideas to give him a name. We had thousands of suggestions ranging from Tweety to Baldy. It was a young lady on the Isle of Arran who won with her suggestion of Rudi. As a point of interest, the Fleetings – a footballing family – named a bar in their hotel in Irvine after Rudi. I was impressed (of course, Rudi didn't drink!).

I did try to introduce another little dachshund called Casper – named after Casper the Friendly Ghost. One day I took him into the studio to try him out in front of the cameras and see how he fared. Casper was fine until the floor manager decided to have a bit of fun with him. He came up close to the desk and, putting his face close to Casper's, he said 'Master McGrath!' (It was a well-known dog food at that time). Everyone in the studio laughed, except for Casper, who took off at the floor manager as if he were going to eat him there and then. The poor guy didn't know what to do: he moved out of Casper's sight, made it up to him with titbits, and really tried everything to calm him down. All Casper did was bark and bark and bark. I tried bringing him back into the studio but every time Casper saw anyone who looked like that floor manager he began barking again.

Rudi was not a well dog at the end of 1979, and after a visit to our vet we decided home was the best place for him. He had only been going to the studio with me one day a week for recordings of *Cavalcade* but even that, I could see, was a bit of an effort.

Sad to say he made the front page of the *Daily Record* on Thursday, 10 January 1980. The headline read, 'The Best Known Dog in Scotland is Dead', and there was a lovely picture of Rudi.

He used to get mail from hundreds of children during his fourteen years on *Cavalcade*. There were more than a few tears in our family, I can tell you. Anyone who has a dog will know exactly what I mean. He was fifteen years old and we had lost a member of our family. The house seemed so quiet without him and so it wasn't long before we all set off for the kennel in Thirsk to try to find another companion for the family – and maybe even the TV programme.

We were in luck. The kennels had recently had a happy event and when we arrived we were presented with a problem. Have you ever had to choose one out of six of the most gorgeous-looking, light brown, shaggy-coated puppies in the world? We sat in the kitchen of the house and watched these little bundles of energy skidding around on a highly polished floor. I asked the all-important question: what was their temperament like? We were taken out to the main kennel to see their mum and dad and they rushed towards us, tails wagging, both obviously as happy as Larry.

We'd left our son Christopher in the kitchen, watching and playing with the puppies while we took a peek at their mum and dad. I'm very glad we did as it was Chris who had the last word – this was to be his selection. Without any hesitation Chris pointed out one pup in particular. I asked him why he'd picked on that one. It was sitting down watching all the others rushing around frantically. Chris said he'd been doing the same as the others then, suddenly, he'd stopped, and looked around as if to say: 'What on earth are you all rushing around for?' He ran over to Chris when he clicked his fingers at him, wagging his tail furiously in greeting. So that was it. One tiny puppy had a home. There was never any question about a name for our new member of the family. It was to be Rusty (again).

My wife had a shop in Prestwick at the time and when we got him home he was never left on his own. Beryl took him to the shop and he was, I believe, as good as gold apart from eating the odd trinket! She trained him in between serving customers – not an easy task.

After a while I thought I'd try and see if he would fit into my TV show. I took him up to the studios one transmission day and introduced him to the cameras and the children at home. Rusty was an instant hit and from day one was a star. He took to the cameras like an artist who'd been working in television all his days. I would take Rusty into the studio and we would rehearse the show. Then when it came to recording we would have to do it all over again. Rusty would sit on my left on the *Cavalcade* desk and react to everything I did. He was wonderful – a man's and a presenter's best friend.

As he got older I had him with me all the time. Rusty loved travelling in the car and would sit up beside me in the passenger seat. I remember once driving up to traffic lights in Glasgow on the way to the studios. As I pulled up a motorbike drew up beside me. Now, Rusty had a habit of placing his left front-paw on the arm of the door. Rusty, you have to remember, was a standard, thick-set dachshund with a long body and lots of wiry, shaggy hair. But sitting up straight – literally sitting on his bottom – was no problem at all to him, unlike most dachshunds. This feat was supposed to be almost an impossibility for the breed. He'd also developed a habit of smiling. If you looked at him he'd throw his head back and give you the widest grin ever showing his pearly-white teeth. Some people who didn't know him might think he was snarling. However, our friend on the motorbike was bored with having to wait at the lights and was looking around for something to interest him. He glanced at my passenger and did a double-take – he couldn't believe what he was seeing. It was a little unfortunate because Rusty, thinking no doubt that he was a fan of *Cavalcade* – decided at that precise moment to give our motorbike friend one of his widest trademark smiles. It's not every day you see a dog sitting up like a human in passenger seat of a car in the centre of Glasgow in the middle of the day. When the lights turned green, the motorcyclist was still gaping at Rusty, and fell off his bike with shock. Our line of cars sailed on leaving him stranded in the middle of Hope Street.

I've never told anyone before, but once I actually lost Rusty. After a recording of *Cavalcade* I was a little unsure about my performance, so I decided to go and look at a replay in the control room. The studio was left in darkness and after viewing the show on tape I made my way back to my dressing room when I suddenly realised Rusty wasn't with me.

211

Panic!

Where was he? What had I done?

I dashed back down to the blacked-out *Cavalcade* set and switched some lights on, to find Rusty fast asleep in his usual spot on my desk, exactly where I'd left him some considerable time before. He wasn't in the least bit bothered and simply wagged his tail in welcome when he heard me approaching and licked me.

Rusty did so many things that made him extra special as a family pet and a TV star of the first order. He did so much for charity and we went to hospitals, children's homes and so on. He even led parades with pipe bands, though he absolutely hated the bagpipes.

He also came out with me on Road Shows and he would do what I called his footballer act. Rusty was never formally trained in anything but just picked quirky things up extremely quickly. He was a real show-business dog. I discovered Rusty could be a first class goalkeeper quite by chance. I had taken him to a show and as usual everyone was mobbing him. I left him on stage to go down and into the audience where someone gave me a tennis ball and told me it was a present for Rusty. On the spur of the moment I threw the ball towards Rusty who was looking down at me from the stage. I shouted 'Catch' and Rusty did more than catch. He hit the fast-moving tennis ball with his nose and it came flying back to the audience. I was amazed. I looked at him on stage wagging his tail like mad as the audience applauded. They thought it was part of the act. I picked up the ball thinking what he'd just done was a fluke. Rusty's eyes met mine, and then went to the ball in my hand. He began running up and down the front of the stage and was obviously waiting for me to throw the ball again. I showed the ball to him and he stood stock-still, watching my every move. I lobbed the ball in an arc. He kept his eyes on the ball and jumped to meet it in mid-flight. Once again he hit it with his nose and once again it came back into the audience. I couldn't believe it. I kept lobbing the ball to Rusty and as many times as I did this he would hit it back to me, thoroughly enjoying every moment of this improvised act. Rusty left the stage to great applause.

Sometimes I had to go to London for meetings and I travelled by car because we always took Rusty. He loved the car. When in London we always stayed at the Basil Street Hotel near Harrods. Our first visit to the hotel was amusing. I walked into reception fully expecting them to say 'no dogs allowed'. Instead, I was greeted by a young man who didn't look at me but leaned over the reception desk and said: 'And what brings *you* to London, Rusty?'

After plenty of laughter we signed in and he told us he'd watched *Cavalcade* as a child. I was delighted – even more so on arriving in our rooms to discover flowers and a card of welcome. As Tommy Cooper used to say: 'Just like that.' It was pretty impressive to have organised this so speedily as we hadn't pre-booked our accommodation. We returned there several times after that welcome. I was always amazed when in London that so many people knew Rusty. I often wondered if I should take Paladin with me as well.

Many people still ask me how Paladin came to be introduced to *Cavalcade*. To tell you the truth, it was really just by sheer chance. I was viewing some cartoons when I came across one with Bugs Bunny, a magic lamp and a genie. This scenario played at the back of my mind for a few days and I couldn't shake off the idea of a lamp and a genie. Then I thought of having a genie as a pal and it suddenly clicked. I would have a very old lamp as a friend to talk to on my *Cavalcade* desk. But how would he speak? What would he sound like? And what sort of a lamp would he be? I used to collect the odd antique, so I thought, why not an oil lamp? Someone would live in the lamp and have a voice. And who would live in an old lamp? It had to be an old man. In fact, it had to be an old Scottish man in an old Scottish oil lamp.

First, I had to get a suitable voice. I tried doing it in a Highland lilt. After a chat with the sound department, I settled for sticking my head into a wastepaper bin and we tried recording the voice. It worked well – there was a good echo coming from the bin. We were off. As the weeks went by I noticed the voice I started off with was getting a little gruffer, a little deeper, and much more Glaswegian. From then on, the wastepaper bin would produce the voice of a grumpy old man from Glasgow. Paladin was finally born.

I would write the script then record Paladin's lines, leaving a gap so that I would be able to say my lines live on the show. It had to be spot-on or it didn't work. If Paladin said his line and I hesitated he would carry on speaking over me and the entire recording would have to stop. Most times I got it right. I used to script it so that he could be cheeky to me at every opportunity and I used to make equally cheeky remarks back.

Over all the years on air I only had one complaint about Paladin and me talking to each other. I was getting a lot of cheek from Paladin during one *Cavalcade* and a few days afterwards I received a letter from a head teacher of a school in Aberdeenshire. It was very polite. His family had enjoyed the show on Grampian TV *but* he objected to the interplay between Paladin and myself. His letter went something like this: 'Last Sunday as we were watching your show as a family, you turned to Paladin and said "shut up". As a father of two children, how can I be expected to bring them up properly when they can hear language like that on a children's programme?' As a matter of fact, I agree with him. I only wonder what he must think of today's television . . .

I know what I think. Pre-school programmes try to be, and are, generally quite good. But programmes aimed at primary school children are so boring. Every format seems to be the same and there's not a great variety of content. Sometimes it seems like if you've seen one show, you've seen them all. The average children's show consists of a couple of young presenters who are encouraged to speak extremely quickly in excitable, high-pitched voices while moving at a demented pace. They give the impression they can't get to the next item quick enough and when they do the whole process is repeated. I don't blame the presenters though. I lay the blame firmly at the producers' door. Oh, for a little calm and variation. I hate it when presenters talk down to kids – they're far too intelligent to be treated like that. Entertain them, for goodness' sake! But don't talk down to them.

Paladin was well established when I introduced another *Cavalcade* cast member: Totty the Robot. By this time we didn't need a wastepaper bin for Paladin's voice. The sound department could change my tones with the flick of a switch. So I also became the voice of Totty, who could move about the studio unaided: unlike old Paladin who, by this time, was feeling his age. Originally, he was hired for ten shillings a week. One day someone noticed this bill. So, after around twenty years, he was paid for outright and became a fully-fledged member of the *Cavalcade* family.

It was in 1975 (before the BAFTA awards) that we won the 'Scottish ITV Programme of the Year Award' from the Radio Industries Club of Scotland, and in 1991 we received a commendation in the Queen Mother's 80th Birthday Awards (as part of the Keep Britain Tidy award scheme). The citation read:

Glen Michael hosts a popular Scottish Television children's programme that is broadcast every Sunday afternoon. He has made a superb effort to stimulate and encourage children to care for their environment by participation in the National Spring Clean and many other local litter prevention activities. Glen Michael's programme identifies with young people and has a high degree of popularity amongst them and has encouraged even more young people to Keep Scotland Beautiful.

The award was presented to me by Princess Margaret at the Russell Hotel in London.

Cavalcade was often on before *Scotsport*, and our handovers gave me a lot of pleasure over the years. I remember linking up with Arthur Montford in the *Scotsport* studio by throwing a football out of shot. The next thing the viewer would see was Arthur catching the ball and saying: 'Thanks, Glen, and welcome to *Scotsport*.' In those days that was really quite clever . . .

On another handover I wore a football top made up of two club colours. The side-hand left was one club's colour and the right was the others.' I wasn't stupid. If I seen to be taking sides I probably would have lost half my viewers just like that! (I'll leave you to guess the two clubs . . .) I remember playing in a charity football match and was thrilled to have Jimmy Johnston of Celtic and Willie Henderson of Rangers in my team. I was sent on as a sub for the last ten minutes and was no sooner on the pitch than I had the ball at my feet. I raced for the goal down the right wing and out of the corner of my eye could see Jinky Johnston flying along on my left keeping in line with me. I looked up to see the goal in front of me, aimed at it – and missed by a mile! On my left Jinky was laughing his head off and quipped: 'You've been watching too many cartoons, Glen.'

There was always a football connection with *Cavalcade*. We once had the great Willie Miller of Aberdeen on the show. He had to demonstrate his ear-waggling ability in a Waggle Your Ears competition that we had running at the time and he did rather well. And then there was the time that Jim Leishman let me film a comedy episode at Dunfermline Football Club when he was manager. We shot some action scenes with the team and me as a goalkeeper. Afterwards I asked if him if he would give me a trial as a goalie. His reply was simple and to the point.

'Don't ring me . . . I'll ring you.'

Away from the world of sport I remember one very unusual moment in the STV studios when George Younger – Secretary of State for Scotland, MP for Ayr, and later Lord Younger – was walking through the *Cavalcade* studios as a short cut to the news studios where he was going to be interviewed live on air. He spotted me at my desk and called a halt to the entourage that surrounded him, insisting on being photographed, not with me, but with Paladin the Lamp. He left my studio roaring with laughter.

That was always the way with *Cavalcade*. It was more than just a children's television programme – it brought whole families together, all ages, united them for just a little while with a bit of fun and laughter. When I think of it now I like to imagine it was just like the old radio programmes I would listen to with my mother and father as a young boy.

It seems such a long way from those early days, my childhood spent always on the move. There was so much uncertainty, but perhaps the constant changes of scenery, all the different faces and places, influenced my young mind and were the making of me as a performer. Who can say? I wasn't born by the side of a stage, my first breath of air wasn't a whiff of grease paint, but I know my heart will always rest in the halls of variety performing. Life is a show full of ups and downs, miseries and joys, crescendos and silence. It never ceases to amaze you, and if you're lucky it will keep you rapt all the way through. Life *is* a Cavalcade.

What more is there for me to say? It feels a little like I'm back in my dressing room after that last show. So I'll stare at the face in the mirror, break into a smile through my make up, and say for one last time: 'I hope you've enjoyed the show. 'Til next time we meet, you take care . . . Goodbye!'

Index

219